ALSO BY CLARE BELL

Ratha's Creature
(A MARGARET K. MCELDERRY BOOK)

Clan Ground

Clan Ground

C L A R E B E L L

A Margaret K. McElderry Book

NEW YORK   1984   ATHENEUM

To my friends,
Dorothy and Donya,
who were there at the beginning.

Library of Congress Cataloging in Publication Data

Bell, Clare.
  Clan ground.

  "A Margaret K. McElderry book."
  "An Argo book."
  Summary: The stranger Orange-Eyes, recognizing that
the one who controls fire can become absolute ruler,
challenges Ratha's authority over the Named, a clan of
intelligent wild cats living twenty-five million years
ago.
  [1. Fantasy.   2. Cats—Fiction]   I. Title.
PZ7.B3889153Cl   1984   [Fic]   84-6289
ISBN 0-689-50304-0

Copyright © 1984 by Clare Bell
All rights reserved
Published simultaneously in Canada by
McClelland & Stewart, Ltd.
Composition by Maryland Linotype Composition Company
Baltimore, Maryland
Printed and Bound by Fairfield Graphics
Fairfield, Pennsylvania
First Edition

Clan Ground

CHAPTER 1

THE GATHERING was to take place in the older part of the meadow, about the flat-topped stone the herders called the sunning rock. Thakur, the herding teacher for the clan, arrived first. With a glance over the meadow to see if anyone else was coming, he bunched his hindquarters and leaped up on the gray stone, then stretched out to catch the sun's last warmth. Insects droned about his ears and a rock lizard hissed at him for taking the best spot. He flicked his tail at the lizard once, then ignored it.

Thakur shifted himself in the slight hollow worn by the many who had lain there before him and felt the sun-gathered heat of the stone through the fur of his belly. He folded his forepaws beneath him and let a soft purr flutter in his throat as the evening breeze ruffled the fur on his back. Then the breeze died away and only the twilight stillness and the scent of the sunning rock rose up about him.

The stone he lay on had its own scent. One couldn't smell it when there were other, stronger odors in the air or a wind blowing, but at other times, one could catch the faint scent of ancient rock baked by sun and beaten by rain.

Thakur's purr grew softer until it faded. He felt slightly ill-at-ease sitting here where Ratha, the clan leader, would be when the clan assembled. He thought of the Firekeepers and the dance-hunt that was soon to come. The sunning rock seemed to cool beneath him and he shivered.

The dance-hunt had begun as a story, a retelling of the clan's battle against the Un-Named Ones who preyed on the herd and drove the clan to the edge of destruction. Bearing a strange new creature called the Red Tongue, a young female led the fight, striking such fear into the raiders that they trampled their own wounded as they fled. Few of the Un-Named had been seen near clan ground since the final battle. By her courage and wit, Ratha had gained clan leadership and the tale was begun to honor her.

The herding teacher was old enough to carry the scars from that fight and to recall how the story had been first told. He also remembered how it changed in the telling. Those who told it added movements to their words and the words themselves became a chant to which the tale-tellers swayed.

In the first cycle of seasons after Ratha's victory, anyone could be chosen to tell and act the story. Later, the Firekeepers, who had been given the duty of keeping Ratha's creature, claimed the honor as theirs. They enlarged it, adding more individuals to play the parts of enemies and defenders. They added more motion, until it changed from an acted tale to a dance.

Much less to Thakur's liking was the way the story changed from triumphant to vengeful and the dancer's motions from joyous to frenzied. Somehow Ratha didn't seem to notice, or, if she did, she thought the change was unimportant. Each season Thakur disliked the dance-hunt ritual more, for it kindled in him a strange fear, one he couldn't put a name to.

Perhaps he felt the fear because his own ties to the Un-Named were too close. Though born of a clan female, Thakur and his brother Bonechewer were sired by an Un-Named male. Clan law forbade such matings and for good reason: they often produced young who lacked the intelligence and self-awareness necessary to a people who called themselves Named. Though Thakur's mother had been exiled for violating that law, the old clan leader had seen the light of the Named in the cubs' eyes and had tried to keep them within the clan. In the end, Thakur had stayed behind, while Bonechewer was taken by his mother to join the Un-Named. Because of his parentage, Thakur had never been fully accepted in the clan until Ratha's ascendancy gave him the status to which his abilities entitled him.

The high grass parted far across the meadow and he heard the noise of other herders and the sound of herdbeast carcasses being carried and dragged. The clan would feast well before the dance-hunt. They had chosen a three-horn doe and a big stag, one almost too heavy for the jaws that held it.

He watched the herders come across the meadow, their fawn and golden brown pelts melding into the colors of the dry grasses. His own coat was a dark coppery shade not common among those of the clan.

Thakur's task of teaching clan cubs to manage dapplebacks and three-horns didn't include helping to cull the animals. Sometimes he did help, for the younger herders often needed skill and experience as well as raw strength. But Thakur was willing to let the others do the killing.

Many herdbeasts have felt my teeth and there will be more, he thought. *I have grown old enough to know each animal I take and to sorrow as much as rejoice in its death.*

When the herders drew near, they waved their tails at him to come and help drag the carcasses the last distance to the sunning rock. The rich smell of meat coaxed Thakur down off his perch. He hurried to seize a dragging hock, for he knew that those who helped to carry the culled beasts would be among the first to eat. Of course Ratha came before any of them, but she always left plenty.

The order in which the clan ate would change tonight, for the Firekeepers needed to keep their bellies empty to meet the exertion of the dance-hunt. The second animal the herders had culled would be saved to feed the dancers.

By the time all the clan herders had their turn at the first kill, twilight was past and the stars shone overhead. Despite his uneasiness, Thakur had eaten well and carried a rib bone away with him to crack and lick while he waited for the dance-hunt to assemble. Hunger was not so strong in his mind now as it had been earlier, and, as he savored the salty marrow, he remembered the Un-Named raider that he and the other herders had chased away that morning. Near clan ground the Un-Named were few and widely scattered, but every once in a while one or two would come on their land, driven by drought and poor hunting.

Thakur didn't know why this Un-Named One had come. The stranger had lacked the strength to try for even the weakest dappleback. He was so starved that he looked like a yearling, although the length of his teeth and his ragged silver-gray coat told Thakur he was older. The herding teacher remembered the stranger's face, a face so drawn that bones of cheek and jaw showed under the sparse pelt. *I hope these three-horns were slain downwind of the Un-*

Named One. It would be cruel of us to make him smell what he may not eat.

Several Firekeepers passed Thakur, carrying kindling in their jaws. They threaded a path through the clanfolk, leaving the scent of pitch pine on the evening breeze. He watched them arrange the wood in a pile and depart to fetch more. Thakur's teeth ached at the thought of their task and he felt glad he taught herding.

He listened to the sound of grunting and crunching nearby as powerful jaws cracked a stag's thighbone. He worked his own piece of rib around to the side of his mouth and chewed it absently. The herder next to him, who had broken the thighbone, sat up stiffly, his nose raised and his whiskers back.

"What's in the wind, Cherfan?" Thakur asked, knowing his neighbor by the latter's scent. Cherfan stiffened again and lay down. "I thought I caught a whiff of that raider we chased away."

The herding teacher tested the breeze and found only the familiar smells of clanfolk. "Your nose must be playing tricks on you. That Un-Named One barely escaped us. He wouldn't be able to drag himself this far. If he isn't dead yet, he will be in a few days."

"And I'll be the one who has to carry him away. Phew! I get all the smelly jobs," Cherfan grumbled and then added, "Look, there's Ratha."

A slim shape padded across the starlit meadow and leaped to the top of the sunning rock. At her arrival, the gathering grew quiet. Mothers hushed restless cubs and those chewing on bones put them aside. Several Firekeepers left bearing branches in their mouths, and Thakur knew they had gone to light their brands at the dens where the fire-creature was kept.

Across the dark grass, Thakur saw the flickering light of torches. Far away as they were, the approaching firebrands seemed to challenge the cold light of the stars. In the gathering circle, heads turned and eyes glowed red at their centers. A soft wail started up from many throats. It grew louder and gained rhythm as the firebearers drew nearer. The wails and howls joined into a worldless song that praised the Red Tongue. Thakur felt the cry welling in his own throat and clamped his jaws together to stop it.

Now the gathered faces were lit; shadows fled across the pale grass as if they were live creatures that dreaded the coming of the power the clan called the Red Tongue. As the shadows of tree and bush escaped into the lair of night, other forms, hidden beyond the approaching firelight, crept toward the torchbearers.

Two odors came to Thakur from two different directions. From the Firekeepers came a sharp, excited smell, an aggressive scent that stung his nose as much as the smoke from their brands. From the others, the mock enemy in the dance, came a bitter smell that brought acid into the back of his throat and dried his tongue.

The dance-hunt began. The torchbearers leaped into the center of the circle and the fire seemed to fly with them. Their faces were visible now, their muzzles outlined against the fierce light of their brands. At the opposite side of the circle, those who had no fire froze and flattened in the grass.

Thakur felt his neck fur prickle. *Every time I see this, I have to remind myelf it is not a real fight. I wish they didn't do it so well.*

One of the torchbearers crossed the open ground before the sunning rock and swung his brand down to light the brush pile at its base. From the "Un-Named" side came snarls and someone leaped with forepaws flung apart, mouth open and red.

The torchbearer started and shied, pulling back his brand. Another "enemy" sprang onto him, dragging him down by his hindquarters. His firebrand fell and smoked. The clan's wail died to a hiss. The Firekeepers charged, routing the raiders, pushing them into the darkness. But soon their opponents crept back and attacked once more.

The clan's song rose and fell, becoming a wordless chant that followed the pace of the battle. As the torch-bearers stalked their night-hidden opponents, the voices hushed to a murmur. At each run and clash, they rose to a shriek.

The battle followed the chant as well, for the Fire-keepers' steps came to that rhythm and those who played the Un-Named crept and flattened to the pulse of the cry. About Thakur, tails swished and paws struck the ground together. He felt himself drawn into the rhythm with every breath he took and every movement he made. He clenched his teeth and drove his claws into the ground.

I saw no harm in this dance when it began as a joyful celebration. But season by season, it has changed into something fierce and cruel.

The fight grew wilder. Some of the Un-Named fell and rolled as if dead. Burns and scratches showed along their sides, beading blood. A new smell tainted the air and Thakur knew that some torchbearers had forgotten that this fight wasn't real. He shifted, flattening his ears. *Ratha, can't you see what the Red Tongue has done to our people?*

He sought the eyes that glowed green from the sunning rock, but she, like the others, was too mesmerized by the dance-hunt to look back at him.

Despite the smell and feel of bodies close about him, Thakur felt isolated. He watched the limp forms that he knew were living, and sweated through his pawpads. He felt as though his fear made a change in his scent that would betray him as half-clan and vulnerable to the hate being howled at the enemy. Beside him, Cherfan sniffed, turning his nose toward Thakur even though his eyes remained fixed on the scene before him. Thakur tried to calm himself, knowing that his neighbors might detect his uneasiness.

In the circle, the battle split apart into individual fights as the Firekeepers stalked the remaining enemy. The combatants whirled, lunged and struck with claws and firebrands. The song and the fight grew fiercer, until the last of the enemy was driven away into the darkness. A panting torchbearer came forward to light the brush pile and Thakur could see it was the Firekeeper leader, Fessran. She tossed her torch into the tinder and flame leaped up.

He heard her voice above the roar and crackle. "Is it well, Tamer of the Red Tongue and Giver of the New Law?"

"It is well, Firekeeper," came Ratha's reply from the sunning rock. "My creature is still strong. It will defend us against the Un-Named as it did when we drove them from clan ground."

Her voice was strong, but it sounded to Thakur as though she had pulled herself from a daze. He wondered if she understood at last the dangers of the ritual that she had created. But whatever thoughts she had then were interrupted as Fessran drew back her whiskers as if smelling some new and threatening scent. She peered intently into the night, suddenly rose from her place at the front of the gathering and left the bonfire.

Ratha sprang to her feet. For an instant, she looked puzzled, then her gaze followed Fessran's and her tail began to wag angrily, challenging the intrusion. "Hold, Firekeeper!" Ratha cried, staring into the darkness beyond the circle. "The hunt is not finished."

Silence swept across the clan as all eyes followed her gaze. Another smell filled the air, pungent and sour. It spoke of desperation mixed with fear in the form of a stranger who still lurked outside the circle. All Thakur's hairs stood on end, for he knew by the scent who the intruder was. Around him other herders bristled in response to the invasion.

Quietly the herding teacher left his place, circling around the outside of the group. He saw Cherfan and Shoman plunge into the night after the intruder. When Thakur had almost caught up with them, Cherfan reappeared tailfirst, his teeth fastened in a bony leg. With one heave the big herder yanked the stranger into the circle of firelight.

The captive made a frantic series of jerks as if he could tear the leg off and leave it between Cherfan's jaws. Then with a hoarse cry, the silvercoat twisted and lunged, his fangs seeking the herder's cheek. Thakur leaped, seized the silver's scruff and pulled his head back. The teeth clicked together in front of Cherfan's face.

Thakur wrinkled his nose at the pungent taste of an ill-kept pelt. He could see Cherfan grimace as fleas jumped from the captive's hindquarters onto the herder's nose. More of the Named sprang on the stranger and a howl went up. The Firekeepers ran to help and were halfway across open ground when Ratha's snarl halted them. "Stop the fight," she ordered. "Bring this stranger to me."

The clan was so fevered from the dance-hunt that the

scuffle continued for a few more moments before it finally stopped. Thakur lost his hold on the stranger's ruff and backed out of the fight. The herders Shoman and Cherfan emerged from the fray dragging the tattered form of the Un-Named One. There was more red than gray on his fur now. Shoman wrenched him back and forth, tearing his ruff. With an angry grunt, Cherfan pulled the Un-Named One from Shoman's jaws and dragged him to the sunning rock. The torchbearers surrounded him with their brands so that Ratha could see him. The captive squinted and shut his eyes against the fierce light.

Thakur shook his head and smoothed the fur ruffled by the fight. *This morning he was too weak to be a danger to the herdbeasts. Now he has asked for death by coming here.*

The torchbearers pulled back their brands and the captive's eyes opened. Thakur looked into them, expecting to see a dull green or yellow stare clouded by panic, and the inability to understand. He had seen it before: the gaze of animals who resembled the Named in every way except for the lack of light in their eyes.

The herding teacher flinched in surprise at what he saw. The Un-Named One's eyes shone orange. Not amber, but a deep, glowing orange, the color at the center of the Red Tongue. In the depths of those eyes, almost masked by rage and fear, was a clarity and intensity Thakur hadn't expected.

Others of the Named had seen it too. Suddenly the invader had become more than a scavenging animal.

Thakur saw Ratha lean so far down from the rock he thought she might tumble off. Slowly the Un-Named One lifted his muzzle to meet her stare. The silvercoat opened his mouth and Thakur tensed, ready to spring to Ratha's aid if the Un-Named One attacked her.

What came from the stranger's jaws was not a roar of challenge nor a whimper of fear, but words in clan speech.

"Not bite. Not claw," he said in a hoarse voice. "Came to clan. Not to kill."

The words were awkward and ill-spoken, but understandable. This time Ratha did slip and had to scramble to regain her seat. The other clanfolk stared at each other in disbelief.

"No kills." The silvercoat put out a stiff forefoot. "Sniff paw. No deer-smell. No horse-smell. No blood." He kept the leg extended, although it trembled from weariness.

No one else moved. Thakur saw Ratha look toward him. "Herding teacher, you know the scents of our animals better than anyone else. Tell me if what he says is so."

As Thakur approached the crouching silvercoat, she added, "If there is even a trace of a herdbeast's scent on him, he will die now by my fangs."

The herding teacher circled the Un-Named One, smelling him carefully from all sides and trying to ignore the stench from filth and festering sores. He pawed dirt away from between the toes so he could smell the soil without the other's odor intruding. When he finished, he stood back and said, "He has eaten only roots and grubs. There is no herdbeast smell on him."

Ratha peered down at the orange-eyed silvercoat. "So Thakur says you have made no kills on clan ground. Why have you come here?"

"Clan is fierce and strong. Clan eats while Un-Named grow thin and die. This one, Orange-Eyes, not ready to die."

The hostile muttering faded. The Un-Named One

glanced about. "Orange-Eyes is clever, like clan. Not afraid. Should be with clan." Boldly he added, "Clan needs Orange-Eyes."

Ratha recoiled and spat. "We have no need for a mange-ridden scavenger who thinks too much of himself."

"Orange-eyes has sores because no food. Eating will make better."

"I told you we don't want you. Now go."

The Firekeepers drew their brands aside to let the Un-Named One slink away, but he turned instead to Ratha. "Now this one wants only to die by clan fangs. Let ugly herder with kinked tail come forward and kill Orange-Eyes."

"Gladly," Shoman growled from the back. Thakur felt Shoman push past him roughly, leaving his fur rumpled.

"Shoman, keep your place!" Ratha narrowed her eyes at him, then at the Un-Named One. "So you think you are clever and brave enough to join us." She raised her head. "Fessran, the dance-hunt is unfinished. Let the Firekeepers take their place."

Again the ritual started, the quarry now a single enemy. At Ratha's order, not a claw touched Orange-Eyes, but the torchbearers' steps took them close to him, and they thrust their brands at him, flaunting the Red Tongue's power. Each time a flaming torch came near the Un-Named One, he jumped and shuddered, but he held his ground. The Firekeepers' lunges came closer until fire licked silver fur. Orange-Eyes fell on his side, no longer able to keep his balance, but he refused to either flee or cower.

Fessran, sitting next to Thakur, never took her eyes from the stranger. Her tail curled and twitched with suppressed excitement.

"Enough!" Ratha cried.

The torchbearers fell back. The silvercoat crept to the base of the sunning rock. Thakur heard the murmurs around him and knew that the stranger's courage had impressed even those who bore the greatest hatred for the Un-Named.

The silver lifted his streaked and smeared muzzle to Ratha and stared directly into her eyes. "Orange-Eyes is worthy. Orange-Eyes stays."

She crouched on the edge of the rock, her lips drawn back to show the tips of her fangs. For a moment Thakur thought she would pounce on the Un-Named One and shred the rest of his face for his impudence. As green and fire-colored eyes met, Thakur saw in Ratha's gaze a reluctant and surprised admission of respect. There was a further moment of tension between them; then she wrinkled her nose at the stranger and relaxed.

"All right, Orange-Eyes is worthy," she said. "He stays, at least for now." She got to her feet, cutting off the mutters and growls of astonishment and outrage. "The gathering is ended. The Firekeepers may eat now. To your dens, the rest of you. There are still beasts to herd and day will come soon."

She waited until the group had begun to disperse before calling, "Thakur, come to the sunning rock."

His tail curled in surprise. Ratha jumped down and stood beside Orange-Eyes. The Un-Named One had regained his feet, but only by leaning heavily against the base of the rock.

"Clan teacher," Ratha began, "since you have the most patience of any of us, I ask you to take charge of him for the night. Give him some meat from the Firekeepers' kill and show him the stream where he may wash the blood away. If he is still alive tomorrow, bring him to my den."

CHAPTER 2

RATHA DRIFTED up out of deep slumber. She became aware of the damp, chilly ground under her chin. She squirmed further back into her den, into the warmth still held by dry leaves and grass, leaving only her nose poking out into the early morning wind. When the breeze died, the sun bathed her muzzle and dried the dew on her whiskers. She was slipping back into sleep again when a cold shadow fell across her face.

She came awake instantly, jerking her head up and pulling her paws beneath her. She squinted at the two figures who stood against the sunrise. One she recognized as Thakur, but the other she couldn't place. Who was this skeleton with such a ragged pelt and strange long fangs? Then she caught the stranger's pungent stink and winced.

"Last night," said Thakur's voice softly. Ratha didn't need his words to remember.

"You're early," she grumbled, crawling from the den and trying to smooth her rumpled fur with her tongue. She was further disconcerted when neither of her visitors said anything. They waited while she stretched and groomed. She found herself taking longer than she usually did, for the stranger's direct gaze irritated her.

"I see he survived the night despite the Firekeepers' games," she said to Thakur, allowing her tail one irritable wag. She saw his ears swivel back slightly and she imagined what he must be thinking. *The Firekeepers' game? No, Ratha, the dance-hunt is yours and you gave the order for it to continue.*

At least he had the tact not to speak the thought aloud. She shook her head, making her ears flap. Had she really turned her victory celebration into a test of courage for the Un-Named One? And had she promised him he could stay with the clan as a reward for enduring the Red Tongue's terror? She groaned softly to herself. *I was half-mad last night. I think we all were.*

She sat up, curling her tail over her feet. "Bring him here and let me look at him." She immediately regretted her request when Thakur led his charge in front of her. The full sunlight did nothing to disguise his appearance and seemed to intensify his smell. New blisters overlay old mange and along his ridged back and sunken flanks ulcers showed from festering fly bites. Where parasites and fire hadn't ravaged him, there were the bites and scratches from the frenzied Firekeepers.

Ratha felt sick and ashamed. Driving him away or giving him an honorable death would have been better than unleashing the torchbearers on him. *He would have died last night had I not seen the light in his eyes. Why didn't you die*, she thought at him sulkily. *Then I wouldn't have to bother with you.*

She caught the scent of medicinal herbs and knew that Thakur had applied a chewed-leaf poultice to the Un-Named One's burns. They probably looked and smelled better than they would have otherwise. *Thank you for showing him some kindess, Thakur.* She looked at the herding teacher and felt her gaze soften.

"Lie down if you want," she said to the Un-Named One.

He dropped his hindquarters, but the rest of him remained upright. Ratha felt irritation creeping up on her again. She pressed her tail under one hind foot to keep it from wagging. Every look and move the stranger made seemed softly defiant. Inside that starvation-ravaged carcass, she could see the build of a powerful young male, and she found herself wondering what sort of opponent he would be at his full strength.

"Do you still wish to join us?" she asked.

"Orange-Eyes came to join clan. Is all Orange-Eyes wants, leader."

"Here in the clan we use names when we speak to each other. You know Thakur. I am Ratha. You will also be given a clan name if you stay with us."

"Will take clan name and learn clan ways, Ratha-leader." The silvercoat flinched at his mistake and added, "Is not 'Ratha-leader' but 'Ratha,' yes?"

She relaxed. He was trying to please. Perhaps his defiance was all in her own mind.

"Yes." She took her foot off her tail.

"I'll take him to the meadow with me and he can watch while I teach the cubs," Thakur offered. He turned to the Un-Named One. "Do you feel strong enough?"

"Legs still . . . ," the other said, groping for a word. He raised a paw and flailed it, giving Ratha a rueful grin.

"Shaky," Thakur supplied.

"Legs still shaky, but belly much better. Not learning bad for Un-Named One, yes?"

"Yes, you do seem to be learning quickly," Ratha agreed. "All right, Thakur. Take him with you. If you want more leaves for his burns, I found a new patch by the stream near the meadow trail."

"Good. I've nearly stripped my old one bare."

Something small and active jumped from the Un-Named One's pelt and landed near Ratha's foot. She hopped away as he scratched himself.

"I suggest, Thakur, that you make him roll in the flea-bane before you do anything else, or we'll all be scratching."

During the next few days, curiosity nagged at Ratha despite her trust in the herding teacher. It was too soon to tell how Orange-Eyes would take to life among the Named. Thakur did say that his strength was coming back and he displayed a sharp interest in the teaching sessions, but as the days went by, she itched to see for herself.

Meetings with the Firekeepers and minor disputes over whose den was dug too close to whose kept Ratha busy. This morning she decided to creep away before anyone else could find her.

The day was bright and hot. Sun and shade dappled the trail through the broken forest to the meadow. Birds flew from oak to scrub thorn, dipping so low over the trail they nearly brushed her back. When she reached the meadow, she made her way through the dry grass, craning her neck to peer above the waving stems and spot the herd. There it was; a small flock of three-horns and dapple-backs that the herding teacher had taken from the larger herd in order to exercise his students.

Thakur and the yearling cubs stood together on one side of the flock. The youngsters gathered around him, their ears cocked, their spotted rumps squashed together, their short tails lifted. He was explaining something; she could hear the rise and fall of his voice, but couldn't understand what he was saying. The cubs seemed attentive. No. Wait. Wasn't one missing? Where was Drani's son Bundi?

Ratha scanned the meadow for a glimpse of spotted fur. There he was, the foolish litterling! Making feints at a three-horn fawn while he should have been listening to his teacher.

And who was that lying in the shade of a scrub oak? The Un-Named One, watching Bundi through slitted eyes. Ratha saw him tense and scramble to his feet.

His motion thrust her gaze back to the misbehaving cub, but she could only see a cloud of dust where he had been. She leaped up, straining to catch sight of the cub. A three-horn doe marched out of the rolling haze, her nose-horn lowered and ready.

Ratha's tail and whiskers went stiff as she sought for a trace of the youngster, fearing she would see him down in the grass with a smashed foreleg or jaw. His shrill squeal drew her gaze to the cub, now flattened in the dirt. He backed away from the deer, his nape bristling, his ears flat.

She drew back her lips and caught the sour taste of fear-scent in the wind. Her hindquarters bunched and she launched herself through fibrous grass, feeling it rake her on legs and chest.

No, Bundi! she thought, remembering her own training. *Never show the animals you are afraid . . .*

The deer stalked after Bundi, her head low, fawns bleating at her sides. Even as Ratha begged her body for more speed, she felt she was too far away to help.

Had he been one of the other students, he might have escaped without her aid. She knew Bundi couldn't. He had neither the speed nor agility to evade the three-horn. *Never again will I give Thakur a weakling cub to train!*

She saw the herding teacher stop talking to his students and stare intently at the far edge of the herd, his ears straining forward. Cubs scattered in all directions as he plunged through their midst and dashed toward his threatened student.

The three-horn gathered herself for the savage rush that would leave Bundi writhing in the dirt . . . before Thakur could reach him.

I won't reach him either, Ratha thought with sudden despair. She filled her lungs and roared, "Use your eyes, Bundi! Stare her down! Use your eyes!"

The cub only cowered, too frightened to obey. The grass rippled between the young herder and the deer. A silver-gray head popped up, ears and whiskers back, orange eyes intense. The deer halted and tossed her head, trying to avoid the interloper's gaze. Then, with a whistling snort, the three-horn charged.

Ratha saw only a gray blur as the Un-Named One streaked toward the deer. He threw himself high in the air before the three-horn, his paws spread and his tail flared. The deer skidded and fell back on her haunches. She reared, striking out with cloven forefeet and bellowing her anger. One foot grazed the Un-Named One as he landed. He yowled and scurried a short distance away.

Ratha sprinted toward Bundi. In an instant his terrified squall met her ears and his spotted pelt appeared before her in the rolling dust. Without breaking stride, she snatched him up by the scruff and galloped away with him bouncing in her jaws. He was too heavy to carry any distance, so she dropped him when they were out of range of the three-horn's charge. She looked back for the Un-Named One.

No new wounds showed on his coat although his ribs were still painfully evident and his flanks drawn. The three-horn swung around, now intent on him. He planted his feet wide apart and stared at the deer, forcing her to meet his gaze. She pawed the ground, trying to start a new charge. Now the orange eyes had trapped her. No matter how the herdbeast might throw her head about, she couldn't escape that fiery gaze.

The Un-Named One took one deliberate step toward the deer. Ratha watched carefully. An animal who learned it could defy the herders was too dangerous to keep. If the three-horn doe charged again, she would be clan meat that day. If the Un-Named One could stare her down and break her will, she would live to nurse her fawns.

She saw Thakur come to a halt. He, too, was watching. The deer lifted a hind leg and placed it nervously behind the other. The Un-Named One took another step. The three-horn's defiance broke and she backed away.

"Enough," Thakur said, nudging the silvercoat aside. He took over and soon had the deer in full retreat. With a disgusted bray, the three-horn wheeled and galloped back into the herd. The fawns followed on spindly legs.

Ratha let out her breath. She heard a smaller sound beside her. Bundi flinched when she looked down on him, and she imagined how he must be feeling. Not only had his foolishness gotten him in danger; he had to be rescued by the clan leader. *No, not really*, Ratha thought. *I wasn't the one who stopped the deer in mid-charge.*

"Thakur will chew your ears for your foolishness," she said roughly to the cub, "but at least you're alive."

The herding teacher had taken the Un-Named into a

patch of shade. Ratha trotted across to Thakur with Bundi trailing behind. "Is the Un-Named One hurt?" she asked.

"No, just tired." He turned to Bundi. "Cub, you know what you did. Go over to the side of the meadow and think about it. I'll speak to you later."

CHAPTER 3

A FITFUL WIND blew against Thakur's whiskers. He caught a scent he hadn't smelled all summer: the scent of rain. It was only midday, but the sky above the meadow had started to darken. Thakur lifted his muzzle to the clouds and saw other herders raising their heads.

The herders circled the restless deer and dapplebacks. Thakur joined them in driving the animals together. Dust rose from beneath many trotting hooves and caught in his throat. There was dust in his eyes, between his toes and on his whiskers. His pelt felt dirty and gritty right down to the roots of his hairs. He had given up trying to lick all of it out, for the taste of it on his tongue made him gag and the next day's work would only add more. Everyone in the clan was beginning to look the same dusty color. Even the Un-Named One's silver fur had turned mousy, giving his fire-colored eyes a startling brightness.

The dapplebacks whinnied and bucked as the herders drove them under the old oak, but Thakur knew that, if the storm brought thunder, they would be less likely to bolt if they were sheltered. The three-horns spread out under other scattered trees, whose few dried leaves offered them little of either food or shelter.

Pale sunlight faded as clouds massed overhead. The herders and their animals lost their shadows and the sky's gray deepened. More torchbearers appeared at the trail-head, carrying the Red Tongue and wood to feed it. Thakur saw the Un-Named One trailing behind them, carrying a small bundle of twigs in his jaws. Although Ratha hadn't yet assigned him a task, he had chosen to help the Fire-keepers.

The Un-Named One, who was still called Orange-Eyes for lack of a clan name, delivered his mouthful of wood to the nearest Firekeeper who needed it and joined Thakur near the oak.

"They bring the Red Tongue today early," Orange-Eyes said in answer to Thakur's glance. "Fessran said the herders see bristlemanes and there may be attack before dark." He still spoke awkwardly, but his mastery of clan speech had improved in a surprisingly short time.

They watched the Firekeepers build small piles of kindling at equal intervals around the edge of the herd and set them alight. The torchbearers tried to locate the guard-fires beneath overhanging pine boughs or thorn-bushes that were high enough not to catch and would give some shelter, but several had to be built out in the open.

Soon a wide ring of small flames, each guarded by a Firekeeper, surrounded the deer and dapplebacks. The sharp scent of woodsmoke mixed with the blowing dust and the smell of the coming storm.

Something struck the ground at Thakur's feet, kicking up a puff of dust. A drop hit his nose. Thunder grumbled and the three-horns bleated. A gust of wind came, tearing at the grass and whipping the guard-fires. Firekeepers pawed at the ground around each flame, scraping away the dried weeds and litter so the fire-creature couldn't escape. *They know how hungry the Red Tongue can be*, he thought.

Again he lifted his nose to the sky. It was a smoky gray, with streaks and ripples that moved like the water in a wide, slow river. Rain would be a welcome gift after the parching heat that had lasted past the summer season, but a downpour might kill some of the fire-creatures, opening up a vulnerable place in the ring of defense around the herd. Thakur felt more heavy drops on his head and his ears. This would be no light shower.

The rain fell faster, beating on his pelt. He didn't usually enjoy getting wet but the rain was warm enough to be pleasant and he was dirty enough to welcome a bath. He stretched himself and fluffed his fur letting the rain trickle through to his skin.

Thakur found himself watching the streaks made by the rain on his companion's dusty flank. Orange-Eyes had recovered rapidly from his bout with starvation. His wounds had healed and his mange was receding, leaving a few sparse areas that already bore the fuzz of new fur.

Thakur noticed other things about him as well. The silvercoat's chest was deeper and his forelegs longer than those of the clan, giving his back a slight slope downwards to his tail. His forequarters looked more powerful than those of the Named; his shoulders and neck more heavily muscled. Even the shape of his head was subtly different. He had an odd arch in his skull that began at the crown of his head and flowed down through his broad nose to meet and blend with the backward curve of his fangs.

It was clear to Thakur that part of the stranger's parentage was neither that of the clan nor that of the Un-Named, but a line unknown. Yet, at least one of his parents had given him the gift of self-knowledge that lit his eyes. Would he be able to pass it on to his young?

The rain grew heavier, soaking their coats and turning the dust to mud. Thakur saw several Firekeepers gathered about one of the guard-fires in the open. Some ducked beneath the sheltering pine bough and breathed on the Red Tongue while others piled kindling.

"Have to go bring more wood," the silvercoat said and loped away. He had barely gone when Thakur heard a strange howl. He turned his whiskers outward from the herd in the direction of the sound. At first the cry was faint and lost in the constant beat of the rain, but it continued rising, gaining strength until it filled the meadow. The eerie, wavering howl broke into barks and yips that seemed to taunt the herders and the Firekeepers as they worked to protect their animals.

The howl faded, leaving only the hiss of the rain. Thakur retreated beneath the boughs of the old oak, water streaming from his tail and ears. The air under the tree was dank and heavy with the noise and smell of wet dapplebacks. In a while Orange-Eyes reappeared at the trailhead into the meadow, delivered his mouthful of sticks and joined Thakur. Many of the other herders also sought shelter from the downpour, although some aided the Firekeepers in trying to protect the guard-fires.

"Dung-eating bristlemanes!" growled the herder Cherfan, spraying his companions as he shook his heavy pelt. "It's not the rain that makes me shiver; it's those howls."

"How many of them did you see?" asked Thakur.

"A pair, but I smelled more. There may be a whole pack. How I hate the stink of those belly-biters!"

As if the enemy had heard Cherfan's words, the howls started again. They were louder this time and wilder, breaking into bursts of short, frantic cries that were unlike any other sound made by animals the Named knew. To Thakur, they had the sound of madness. He felt as though he could no longer stand and listen. "I'm going to help the Firekeepers," he told Orange-Eyes, and dashed out from beneath the oak.

He narrowed his eyes against the sheeting rain and headed for the farthest guard-fire, which had begun to gutter and smoke beneath the canopy of branches held over it by the Firekeepers. He saw Fessran there, fighting to keep the flame alight. She started and shivered as another burst of wild howling broke across the meadow.

"No!" she snarled, slapping a branch from the mouth of a Firekeeper. "That won't do. It's much too green and too wet." She turned to another Firekeeper, a young female with a red-brown coat. "Bira, get a pinewood torch from the nearest fire-lair." She glanced over her shoulder at Thakur. He heard Orange-Eyes canter up behind him as Fessran said, "Herding teacher, you could help by bringing more dry kindling. Take Orange-Eyes with you; he knows where the woodpiles are."

Bira dashed off toward the den where the master fire was kept, and Thakur turned to Orange-Eyes. Before he could repeat Fessran's request, the silvercoat said, "I know what she needs. Follow me, herding teacher."

As Orange-Eyes sprang away, Thakur saw Fessran lay back her ears at another luckless Firekeeper. "Can't you hold that branch so that it doesn't drip right on the Red Tongue? No wonder the creature is dying!"

Thakur peered through the rain, made out the form of Orange-Eyes, ducked his head and galloped after him.

When they reached the woodpile, a heap of broken branches thrown against the base of a large fir, Orange-Eyes began to pull the top ones off.

"The sticks underneath are dry," he said quickly. Thakur forced his muzzle in among the piled branches, ignoring thorns that raked his face. He smelled the warm resinous aroma of wood that had been drying all summer. He fastened his jaws on a branch sticking out from the bottom of the pile and pulled until he thought his fangs would break.

With a sudden snap, the branch came free and he tumbled backwards into a puddle. He felt the clammy ooze soak through his fur to his skin as he scrambled to his feet, but he managed to keep the wood from getting soaked.

To keep the rest of the wood covered, Orange-Eyes replaced the sticks he had taken from the top of the pile. He wrapped his bundle of sticks in a large dock leaf before taking it into his mouth, and showed Thakur how to do the same. When the herding teacher was ready, they galloped back through the rain toward the dying guard-fire.

Thakur saw the blurred forms of Bira and another Fire-keeper pacing alongside her with a pine bough held above the torch she carried. But it was already too late. He heard a despairing yowl above the rain and caught sight of Fessran deserting her fire-creature's nest. For an instant he was puzzled; then he knew that the guard-fire had died and they were trying to save the next one.

He and Orange-Eyes changed direction and galloped to Fessran with their loads of thornwood. Ratha was there, helping the Firekeepers, but despite the new torch Bira had brought the guard-fire began to smoke and faded quickly to embers. They retreated to another blaze that was still alive.

Thakur passed the wood he had brought to the jaws of a Firekeeper and rubbed his muzzle against his foreleg to ease the sting of a scratch on his jowls.

"Go tell Cherfan to drive the three-horns under the oak with the other animals," Ratha said to him. The rain ran down her face, streaking the soot on her muzzle. Behind him he heard Fessran roar in alarm, "The dapplebacks! They're attacking the dapplebacks!"

As Thakur backed out of the choking haze, he saw a line of hunched forms lope from beneath the trees at the meadow's far side. They galloped past the ashes of the dead guard-fires and toward the herd of horses. He could hear their shrill, excited yips.

Ratha bunched her hindquarters and sprang away, followed by Fessran and several Firekeepers. Thakur wheeled and sprinted after them. He felt mud spray his legs and found Orange-Eyes running alongside of him. Ahead were the bristlemanes, a full pack of them. He caught the flicker of Ratha's fawn coat through the rain as she dashed to cut them off.

Her attack split the pack of marauders. Half of them ran past her, heading for the dappleback herd. She and the Firekeepers gave chase and disappeared into the rain. Fessran plunged after her, only to slide to a sudden stop. There were shadows in front of her, shadows turned gray by the rain. Thakur saw the Firekeeper lunge and slash with her foreclaws. The bristlemanes retreated, but not far. They started to close about her again with hungry whines.

Together Thakur and Orange-Eyes charged them. The

animals loped away, their tongues hanging and their short, ragged tails tucked between their legs. Instead of scattering, the bristlemanes circled back. Thakur spun to seek a retreat only to find himself blocked in every direction. He, Fessran and Orange-Eyes were completely surrounded.

He backed up against the two others, smelling their fear and feeling them shake. The downpour grew heavier, until he could barely see a tail-length ahead or hear the faraway cries of the other herders. He felt the fur on his neck rise in fright. The three of them would get no help from the other herders, who must be busy chasing the other raiders from the herd.

The bristlemanes closed in. Now he could see the black and yellow mottling on their pelts and the stiff, coarse manes along their necks. Their eyes shone cold and eager. The flesh of the Named could fill those bellies as well as herdbeast meat, Thakur knew. Their nostrils widened and their large ears trembled, swiveling forward.

The bristlemanes approached cautiously, their black muzzles lowered, their heavy jaws slavering. Their smell reached him, making him think of flies crawling over white bones. The Un-Named One's growl sounded on one side of him, Fessran's snarl on the other. Her snarl turned to a screech as a bristlemane dived for her flank. Thakur saw her twist away and fasten her teeth in the thick mane, but the fur was so stiff and heavy that, however she worked her jaws, she couldn't bite deeply enough. Blood began to run, but the creature stayed on its feet, dragging Fessran with it.

Thakur had to guard himself as another bristlemane rushed him and snapped at his belly. He sprang onto the creature's back, sinking his teeth into its neck. The bristlemane strained its head back, shoving against his jaws until they ached. Teeth clamped on his tail and a savage jerk nearly dragged him off.

He fell to the side, his forelegs wrapped around the creature's neck as he sought frantically for a throat hold. The pull on his tail dragged his hindquarters loose and he heard the shrill cries of the other bristlemanes as they danced around him. He lost his grip and fell heavily on his side. Paws stepped on his flank and noses snuffled at him.

For a moment he could see only legs and bellies. The nearest set of legs shuddered and then staggered. The bristlemane went down with Orange-Eyes on top of it.

Thakur was near enough to see every detail. The silver-coat flung his head back and his lower jaw dropped close to the underside of his throat freeing the full length of his fangs. His head drove down, the teeth descending with the full weight of the Un-Named One's forequarters behind them.

There was a tearing and grinding as teeth sheared through fur and hide to meet bone. The bristlemane screamed once.

Orange-Eyes lifted his muzzle from the ruin of the animal's nape. Thakur stared at him, caught in a sudden cold fright stronger than his fear of the bristlemanes. He knew that the stabbing bite he'd seen was like nothing the Named had ever used.

He pulled himself from his daze as he regained his feet, becoming aware that the other bristlemanes had retreated, whimpering uneasily. A short distance away, Fessran worried the limp body of another. She gave it one last shake and left it. Thakur did not have to approach to see the mark of Orange-Eyes's bite.

Fessran rubbed against Thakur, still shivering with rage.

She spat and showed her fangs at the marauders. She turned to Orange-Eyes, who was wiping his muzzle on the soaked pelt of his kill, and said, "Thanks, youngster. Those teeth of yours are good in a fight."

The Un-Named One looked at Fessran. His eyes were oddly wary. She didn't seem to notice.

She knows he killed the bristlemanes, Thakur thought to himself. *She didn't see how he killed them.*

"Are you injured, herding teacher?"

It took Thakur an instant to respond to Orange-Eyes's question. "They chewed my tail, but nothing else."

Hoarse brays and shrill barks came through the sound of the rain. "There are more of those belly-biters after the dapple-backs," Fessran growled. "Come on!"

Together, the three of them bounded toward the noise.

The rain lightened, and Thakur could see further ahead. The rest of the bristlemanes had cut into the dappleback herd, trying to separate out an old mare and her late-birthed colt. Her coat was grizzled and her feet worn. Thakur knew the herders had marked the pair for culling, for the colt was sickly. So had the bristlemanes.

They ringed the mare and her offspring, forcing them away from the flock. She fought fiercely to regain it, lashing out with her hind feet. One marauder staggered away with its jaw broken and flopping loose. The others dodged her kicks and began to drive the colt down the meadow, nipping at its hocks. They broke into a fast lope, forcing the young dappleback to canter.

From the opposite direction came Ratha and the Fire-keepers with newly lit torches in their jaws, but they were too far away and the pack was gathering speed.

Thakur lengthened his stride until he was alongside the bristlemanes. He saw Orange-Eyes and Fessran pacing him on the other side, across the backs of the bristlemanes. Encircled by the pack, the dappleback mare and her colt veered from side to side, trying to break through the ring of their captors. The mare's sides heaved and her breath came in heavy grunts. Lather flew from her neck and her eyes rolled.

Thakur felt the breath burn in his chest as he panted. He knew he could outrun the bristlemanes over short distances, but they could travel far keeping this pace. They had already settled into a ground-eating lope that would soon weary the pursuing Firekeepers. If the pack got away with these dapplebacks, they would run the pair until they were exhausted, then harass and nip at the horses until they pulled them down.

He clamped his teeth together and put all his remaining strength into one last sprint. He glanced back to see an ugly muzzle open its jaws behind his tail. He raced ahead, lengthening his lead, knowing he would need every bit of the distance.

He bounced to a stop, kicked himself into the air, spun around and hurled himself broadside into the chest of the pack leader. The impact drove the breath from his lungs. With a choked howl, the bristlemane tumbled, and Thakur felt the animal shudder repeatedly as more of the pack piled into it. He clawed his way up through a confused mass of thrashing bodies and snapping muzzles. He heard shrill cries as the rest of the animals scattered in confusion.

With a triumphant whinny, the old mare sailed over his head and galloped away from the writhing heap of bristlemanes. The colt followed. From the corner of his eye Thakur saw the Un-Named One yank a bristlemane away by its tail and seize another. He didn't bother to kill them but just thrust them aside as he and Fessran opened a path for Thakur. The herding teacher dragged his fore-paw loose and thrust it at Fessran. He yelped in pain as she fastened her jaws on his leg and hauled him out of the fray.

Thakur caught the gleam of fire on wet pelts and knew the Firekeepers had encircled the bristlemane pack. Now that the rain was stopping, the torches remained lit. The bristlemanes huddled together in the center, their ears flattened, their howls turning to whines. Several Fire-keepers brought unlit sticks that had been chewed to a point and sharpened in the flame.

The bristlemanes climbed over and around each other to escape the vengeful creature that surrounded them. A Firekeeper thrust a brand at a trapped animal and it re-treated until it backed into the others and could go no further. Its cries became faster and shriller until they became a terrified wail. It crouched and shuddered, trying to bury its face in its flank.

Something made Thakur glance at Orange-Eyes, who stood just outside the circle of torchbearers. The silvercoat's eyes narrowed and his lips drew back in a half-snarl. It was not the same expression as the Firekeepers wore. Their eyes blazed with vengeance-hunger and a sudden, eager cruelty. Orange-Eyes was looking, not at the fright-ened bristlemanes, but at those of the clan who brandished fire at them.

Thakur remembered that the Un-Named One had also faced the Red Tongue's wrath. He came alongside the silvercoat and softly said, "The mare and colt are still loose. We should help the herders find them."

Orange-Eyes's gaze remained fixed on the scene. A change came over his eyes. Their color grew more intense, and it was not just the firelight on his face.

"The Red Tongue is powerful creature," he said softly to himself.

"The mare," said Thakur, nudging the Un-Named One's shoulder.

"Yes, herding teacher." Orange-Eyes blinked, lowered his head and followed.

They found the mare's scent trail, still strong in the wet grass. Thakur looked back once to see the flames rise and fall. Firekeepers lunged with pointed sticks in their jaws. Yapping and snarling, the frenzied animals charged the ring of torchbearers. One Firekeeper lost his brand and fell back. The cornered bristlemanes attacked again. Yowls mingled with shrill yelps as they broke through the circle, throwing their tormentors aside.

Before either Thakur or Orange-Eyes could whirl around, the pack had fled away into the night. Recovering themselves, the torchbearers gave chase, the flames tossing on their brands. Orange-Eyes leaped to join them, but they had gone and their cries had already begun to fade.

Thakur let his muscles relax. "Come back," he called to the silvercoat. "Let the Firekeepers chase them."

Orange-Eyes hesitated, looking after the disappearing glow of the torches. He muttered something to himself that the herding teacher couldn't hear.

"Are you going to help me track those dapplebacks or not?" Thakur felt his patience going. Orange-Eyes started and swung around, the strange expression still in his eyes. It was half resentment and half something else . . . Thakur didn't know what. A hunger, perhaps. A hunger that would not be sated by meat.

CHAPTER 4

RATHA HALTED the pursuit at the far end of the meadow. She slowed, panting, the cries of the escaping bristlemanes still in her ears. Behind her, the torchbearers' growls mingled with the angry snap of the Red Tongue. She shared their fever; the urge to hunt the enemy down with fang and fire.

Terror had given the bristlemanes the speed to outrun the Firekeepers. Their pack-mates lay dead in the meadow and Ratha knew that those who lived bore scars on their memories as well as their hides that would forbid them from again setting foot on clan ground.

She heard a muffled snarl and the sound of a body being dragged and shaken. She turned to see one of the Firekeepers mauling another dead bristlemane. The long tongue hung out of the stiff black jaws and flopped around with each angry jerk he gave the body.

Ratha watched, letting the sight feed her hunger for vengeance. "Enough!" she cried suddenly. The Firekeeper released the corpse and backed away. She waited, studying the eyes that shone back at her with reflected torchlight, their glow softened only by a fine mist of rain. "Enough," she said again in a low voice. "The herd is safe and the enemy gone. Firekeepers, return with me and rekindle the dead fires."

The torchbearers did as she bid them and soon new flames were burning in the ashes of the old. But they too were small and uncertain. Ratha knew that if the rain fell harder it would quench them as easily as it had the others.

"Give the creature more wood," she told the fire-tenders as she paced from one outlying guard-flame to the next. "Make it strong and fierce."

She stopped, watching two Firekeepers struggling to comply. One brought more wood while the other fed the flame. He crouched a safe distance away from the fire's nest, tossing in twigs with a quick turn of his head. The fire flared briefly as it consumed each twig and then died down.

"No," Ratha said impatiently. "Use larger pieces and place them; don't throw them."

With an uneasy glance at her, the Firekeeper seized a thick branch in his jaws, approached the flame as close as he dared and flipped the wood in. It crashed into the fire, destroying the nest of carefully laid kindling and sending up a shower of sparks.

Ratha shouldered the Firekeeper aside and dragged the branch out. Carefully she coaxed the flattened remains of her creature back to life and, once it was burning steadily on fresh kindling, she gave it thicker wood.

Each time she placed a branch in its nest, the fire-creature's breath blasted her face and stung her eyes with heat and cinders. It roared its rage in her ears, licked at her jowls and threatened to consume her whiskers. She had to force herself to lay the wood in position, however much her jowls hurt or her instincts screamed at her to leap away.

When she finished, she backed away thankfully and rubbed her sooty muzzle against her foreleg. The two torchbearers were watching her with mingled awe and resentment. "That is how it must be done," she said. "If you are quick and sure, you will keep your whiskers."

The Firekeeper who had nearly destroyed the Red Tongue's nest stalked over to the leaping flame with more wood in his jaws. He faced the fire-creature, hesitated and lunged forward. He dropped the branch in and scrambled back, his belly white with wet ash, his eyes frightened and defiant.

"Feeding your creature is not easy when it grows so large and wild," he said with a shudder.

"If you seek to tame the Red Tongue by keeping it small, it will die in the rain," Ratha said, trying to be patient.

"When it is fierce, it eats my whiskers," retorted the Firekeeper. "Look how short they are. I can no longer find my way in the dark."

"If you are thinking only of your whiskers and not of your duty, you will burn yourself. Try doing it the way I have showed you."

"I will, clan leader," he said, but Ratha could see in his eyes and his barely controlled trembling that his wish to obey had to fight his terror of the fire. This fear was not an easy thing to put aside as Ratha knew well.

"The more you practice, the better you will become and then you need not be afraid," she said, trying to smooth the harshness from her voice. The Firekeeper looked back at her as if he knew her words were half a lie, but he said only, "Yes, clan leader."

Ratha jogged away from his guard-fire and went past others, stopping to see how other torchbearers were faring. What she saw was nothing new, but it still filled her with dismay. Despite their training and experience, many of the fire-tenders were timid, approaching their fire with tightly shut eyes and flattened ears. They poked wood into the flame with tentative thrusts and snatched their paws back. The torchbearers' smells told Ratha, in a way that their appearance could not, how little they trusted the capricious creature they had to guard.

The moon shone through a break in the clouds, glimmering on the wet grass in front of Ratha. Ahead, under the oak, the Red Tongue danced and crackled, offering its warmth to several of the Named who had gathered around it. She crept in under the tree, shook herself and found a place near the fire. The lop-eared herder Shoman was there, along with Cherfan and some other weary clan members. Fessran basked on the far side of the fire. Ratha looked for Thakur and Orange-Eyes, but found neither. She settled herself and listened to the conversation between Fessran and Shoman.

"Killing those bristlemanes may save us from having to cull a dappleback," Shoman was saying.

Fessran drew back her whiskers. "You may be able to eat bristlemane meat. If so, you may have it."

"You're too fussy. Meat is meat," Cherfan said and yawned, showing the ribbed roof of his mouth and the back of his tongue.

"To you, perhaps." Fessran lolled her tongue at him. "You can eat anything, you big shambleclaw."

Ratha stretched out her pads to the fire's warmth and let the banter flow over her. This wasn't the first time Fessran had teased Cherfan about his indiscriminate appetite. He seemed to take her teasing with patient humor, as he did everything else.

"Have you seen Thakur and Orange-Eyes?" Ratha asked.

"They're on their way," Cherfan answered. "Thakur said he'd find the mare so I could go and get warm."

"He may be awhile. That old mare has more spirit than I thought. Maybe you shouldn't cull her, Cherfan," Fessran remarked and began washing a muddy paw.

"*Ptahh!* You only want younger meat, Firekeeper," Cherfan teased in return. "She'd be as tough as a bristlemane and you know it."

Shoman looked sourly at Fessran. "You think you deserve better meat than bristlemane, don't you, torchbearer. Well, I don't. You and the other singed-whiskers let too many of the guard-fires die. That's why the bristlemanes got through."

"Bury it, Shoman," Cherfan growled as the Firekeeper stiffened and glared. "You're about as helpful as a tick in the skin. Don't pay any attention to him, Fessran. His tail's been in a kink ever since Orange-Eyes came."

Ratha twitched her ears at the mention of the Un-Named One. She lifted her muzzle from her forepaws and said, "You seem to think well of him now, herder."

"I'll admit I had my doubts about him, but he's a hard worker and not easily frightened. He chewed up several of those belly-biters. I wish I'd seen that!" Cherfan looked at Ratha directly. "I think you made a good decision when you decided not to kill him at the dance-hunt, clan leader."

"I don't—" Shoman began, but he was interrupted by a swat from Cherfan that knocked him over. "Oh, go fill your belly, flop-ears. Maybe your temper will improve."

Shoman retreated, his fur and his dignity visibly ruffled. Ratha heard him pad away and felt herself relaxing. Fessran, however, was sitting up, looking solemn. Presently Cherfan got up and stretched. "One last look at the herdbeasts and I'm off to my den. Too wet a night to sleep out. Remind flop-ears that he has the next watch."

Some of the herders left with him; others went back out to the meadow. One by one the Firekeepers also left until Ratha and Fessran were alone by the fire.

"Firekeeper, if Shoman's words are troubling you, don't worry," Ratha said. "I never listen to him."

"Maybe you should." Fessran's voice was flat.

Ratha looked at her sharply. "What else could you have taught the fire-tenders? The Red Tongue is not an easy creature to care for. I don't want to punish any Firekeeper for failing."

"Punishment would be useless," said Fessran. "I scold them if they forget their training, but punishment is no cure for fear."

"I can see how difficult it is for them. The Red Tongue is often a vengeful creature."

"There is a difference between being careful and being timid. Your creature demands much from us who tend it." Fessran gazed at the flame. "Sometimes I think it has senses, like ours, and it knows when someone is afraid of it. That is when it jumps out and burns our whiskers."

In the flickering light, Ratha could see the white scars on Fessran's muzzle. There were more on the Firekeeper's front pads. She bore a few scars herself and she knew that the Red Tongue's lessons were taught harshly.

"Clan leader," Fessran said and Ratha lifted her gaze from the Firekeeper's scarred forepaws to her face. "I know you have given me as many as can be spared from the duties of herding to train as torchbearers. But the fires died in the rain tonight and they will continue to die if they are kept by those who treat them timidly. I can teach knowledge, but courage is something a cub is born with."

"So you want more of the stronger cubs to train as Firekeepers."

"Yes, and not just cubs. There are those who are grown who have the strength of will the Red Tongue demands," said Fessran softly.

The tone of her voice made Ratha's eyes narrow slightly, although she wasn't sure why.

"Who among the Named would you choose?" she asked.

"Besides you and me, there are few. Thakur is one, but he has chosen not to serve the Red Tongue and I understand his reasons." Fessran paused, and Ratha felt herself being studied. "I would choose the young orange-eyed one whose strength and bravery have shown me that he is well fit for the task. He proved himself a worthy opponent when he stood his ground in the dance-hunt. He has proved it again tonight by the bodies of two bristlemanes that lie in the meadow."

Ratha paused. "He is not of the Named, Fessran."

The Firekeeper's amber eyes widened. "I thought you were going to accept him."

"Not before I call a clan gathering. I want to hear from others before I decide."

"Everyone knows who killed those bristlemanes," said Fessran. "If you called us all together tomorrow, you'd have any agreement you need."

And I haven't forgotten that it was he who stopped a charging three-horn to save a clan cub's life, Ratha thought, but she didn't want to say anything that would encourage Fessran to press her further.

The Firekeeper eyed her. "You know that he has already begun to carry wood for us."

"I don't mind that; it keeps him busy. But I don't want you to teach him anything more until I have made my decision. And tomorrow is too early to call another gathering," she added pointedly.

"The mating season will be here soon," said Fessran. "If you wait too long, I won't be good for doing anything except waving my tail at him. And you won't be in much better shape."

Ratha had to grin at Fessran's succinct appraisal of her own behavior during the period of heat. Her tension eased a little as she retorted, "He's probably too young for courting, you randy queen! All the same, you're right. I will make my decision soon."

Fessran curled a paw up to her muzzle and began washing it. She halted, swiveled her ears forward and got up to feed more wood to the fire. Ratha turned her face outward into the cool of the night to catch the scents of whoever was approaching.

Thakur and Orange-Eyes padded under the oak and settled themselves wearily in the Red Tongue's glow. "That mare must have led you a chase," said Fessran as Thakur licked his paw and scrubbed at the mud on his face. "Cherfan could have gone after her. You both have done your work for tonight."

"And you have too, Fessran," Thakur said, with a brief glance at Orange-Eyes. Ratha detected a faint trace of anxiety in his smell and wondered if it were only the mare that had delayed him. "You dug me out of that pile of bristlemanes."

"And Orange-Eyes!" Fessran burst out. "Ratha, you should have seen what he did to those belly-biters. They thought they had me, and I thought so too, but when he charged in and sank his teeth into that one . . ."

Orange-Eyes shifted, looking uncomfortable. "Firekeeper, Thakur was with me"

"Both of you have earned my praise and more," Ratha answered. "When we cull a herdbeast tomorrow, you, Thakur, will eat after me and then Orange-Eyes will fill his belly. Fessran, you will follow."

Thakur gave Fessran a questioning look.

"You've earned it, herding teacher," she said. "And so has he." She got up and stretched. "I suppose I have too."

"Fessran, get some sleep. And Orange-Eyes," Ratha said. "Thakur, please stay."

After the Firekeeper and the silvercoat had gone, Thakur leaned toward Ratha and asked softly, "Will you tell me what troubles you?"

Ratha turned her head and stared at Thakur, wrinkling the fur on her brow.

"Fessran was asking you to accept Orange-Eyes and make him a Firekeeper, wasn't she?"

In spite of herself, her jaw dropped. "How did you know? Your ears must be keener than I thought. Or I spoke louder than I meant to."

"No, I didn't hear you. I've been around Fessran long enough to know that when she wants something, she chases after it."

"I told her that I haven't decided. If he does stay with us, I don't know whether he should be trained as a Fire-keeper. It's true, Fessran does need some more torch-bearers."

"And you are willing to give her what she wants?" said Thakur with surprise and more than a trace of annoyance. "I thought that if he stayed, he would be trained as a herder."

Ratha fought the feeling of guilt that crept over her at the sound of disappointment in his voice. She felt drained by the bristlemane attack and knew she had not chosen her words as carefully as she should have. She hoped Thakur could sense her weariness and not press her further, but this time, his usual selflessness had been pushed aside by anger. He waited, a subdued glitter in his eyes.

Ratha looked at her toes, the ground, the fire; anything but the questioning green eyes. "Thakur, what else can I do?" she burst out at last. "Fessran says she must have torchbearers who have the strength of will to master the fire they guard. If the fires die, then we of the clan have no hope against the Un-Named or the bristlemanes."

"Has Fessran persuaded you that Orange-Eyes alone would make such a difference?"

"He would teach; he would inspire others to try harder. If any torchbearer would make a difference, I agree with Fessran that he would be the one."

"I have no doubt that he would," said Thakur. "I also have no doubt that Fessran is thinking not only of him but of the cubs he might sire. Perhaps he might father a whole family of cubs strong and brave enough to guard the Red Tongue, if they have wit enough to remember which end of a torch to take in their jaws!"

Ratha couldn't help ducking her head and drawing back her whiskers. She felt lost and uncertain. Where was the patient teacher and friend she thought she knew?

"Thakur, why are you so upset about this?"

Thakur took a long breath. "Before tonight, I would have said it was only because I feared his young would be witless. That is worry enough, but now I have seen something else. I find this hard to explain, but I have seen him looking at the fire and I don't like what I see. Ratha, he is not one of the Named, even though he has enough light in his eyes for a whole litter of cubs."

"I thought you liked him." Ratha was puzzled.

"I can like him and still fear him."

"Fear him! A half-grown cub!"

"One who can rip the nape out of a full-sized bristle-mane?" Thakur said, spacing his words. "No, Orange-Eyes is not a cub. I have seen him looking at the fire, and I sense that in some way he may understand it better than we do."

"Well, then, if he does, maybe he can help us find other ways to manage it." She lifted her chin, trying to recapture her confidence.

"No, Ratha. It's not that kind of understanding. He knows what the Red Tongue has done and can do to us. I have a feeling in my belly that his sort of knowledge may be dangerous."

Ratha felt hot and cold. She wondered whether it was just the fire's breath on one side of her and the night's chill on the other or whether Thakur's words angered and frightened her.

"How? Are you afraid he would seize my creature and use it against me?"

"No. I'm not saying he would do that, or even want to. I am only saying that my belly tells me there is risk in making him a Firekeeper. What the risk is, I don't know."

"That's all you can tell me?" Ratha stared at him in dismay.

"Yes."

"And what if I choose to take the dangerous trail?"

He looked at her for a long time. "Then nothing I can do or say can help you bear the load you may carry along that trail. I do not envy you the journey."

"You can't even offer a little comfort?" she said as he turned away.

"No. I don't seem to be able to do the things I used to," he said bitterly. "The coming of the Red Tongue has changed all of us, even me."

She was silent until he had gone a few paces away from the fire. Swallowing hard, she said, "You still may eat after me at the kill tomorrow."

"If you wish me to," he answered and was gone.

It wasn't just the night's cold that made Ratha creep closer to the fire.

CHAPTER 5

AT THE CLAN GATHERING, Ratha looked down from her place atop the sunning rock to the Named settling themselves below. Again they had fed and again they had come together, but this time there would be talk rather than celebration.

She smelled the rich odor of three-horn flesh. It lingered on the twilight breeze even though the herdbeast was now bones and rags of hide. She had eaten half the liver and left the rest to the others. Usually she gorged herself, but too much meat made her sleepy and muddled her thoughts. She went away from the carcass with her belly half-filled; she knew she needed to think clearly tonight.

She watched Fessran lead in the torchbearers. They looked black against the setting sun. The flame that leaped and danced on their brands seemed born of the sky's red and orange light. The Firekeepers who bore no torches carried wood in their mouths. Under Fessran's direction, they arranged the kindling to the side of the sunning rock and lit the meeting fire.

The firelight grew as the sun's glow faded. Wavering shadows stretched out behind the clanfolk. The eyes that turned up to Ratha held their own fires of green and amber. One color was missing among them; the hue closest to that of the flame itself. ·

The Firekeepers lay together near the blaze. Fessran remained on her feet, searching the gathering. Ratha saw the Firekeeper leader sit down again with a puzzled expression in her eyes. From Fessran, Ratha looked across to Thakur, who was sitting on the opposite side with the herders. The closed, remote look on his face told her why the Un-Named One wasn't there.

The group quieted, leaving the evening to the snap and hiss of the Red Tongue. Ratha stood up, waving her tail to indicate the meeting was to begin. She sat and curled her tail about her feet.

"We of the Named," she said, "have seen many changes. Once we were ruled by the Law of the Named and the power of teeth and claws. Now we follow a new law and a new way." She turned her head toward the meeting fire and the Firekeepers beside it. "Change begets change as do cubs that grow up and have their own young. Now another change has come upon us, and again we must choose whether to accept it or turn it back.

"We have always grown from within," she continued. "In Baire's day and Meoran's too, that was the law. There was no mingling with the clanless ones. But we were different then. We are fewer now. The number of cubs born each season is less. We never dared to seek outside the clan for others, but now one of them has come seeking us. He is Un-Named, but he has the same light in his eyes that we do. The question I must decide is this: shall the Un-Named One be taken among us?"

Fessran raised her soot-stained muzzle. "Tamer of the Red Tongue, I would speak in support of the Un-Named One. I would like him to hear my words. Why is he not here?"

Ratha's gaze darted to Thakur. He seemed to wilt a bit as other stares followed hers. He sighed and sat up. "He is not here, Fessran, because I told him to stay with the yearlings. I thought it best that we make our decision without him." Thakur paused. "Remember what happened during the dance-hunt."

Fessran walked to the base of the sunning rock and looked up at Ratha. "Giver of the New Law, I do recall what happened then and that is why I speak in praise of him. Never have I seen such courage, even among my own torchbearers."

"Firekeeper leader," said Thakur, "you forget that he is neither Named nor of the clan. Our own yearlings may not come to this meeting until they have proven themselves worthy."

But the Un-Named One has proven himself, Ratha thought suddenly. *When he turned back the herdbeast so I could save Bundi, he showed his worth.*

"He can't be treated as a yearling, Thakur," said Fessran. "He isn't one. Ratha said his coming is something new to the clan. It can't be dealt with in old ways." The Firekeeper leader turned again to the sunning rock. "Clan leader, I and the Firekeepers ask that he be allowed into this gathering so he may hear our words."

A surprised murmur rippled through the group and

Ratha caught an undercurrent of growls from the herders. Shoman leaped to his feet, his tail lashing.

"I have no praise for the Un-Named One," the lop-eared herder sneered, glaring at Thakur. "But I join with the Firekeepers and ask that he be brought before us."

Thakur's jaw dropped. His eyes narrowed at Shoman. He looked to Ratha. "Is it the will of the Named?" he asked, his voice sounding harsh.

"Yes, Thakur," she said and saw his eyes frost. "The meeting will wait while you fetch him."

Clanfolk parted to let the herding teacher through. When he was gone, Ratha studied the two others who had spoken: Shoman, with his lip curled and his whiskers drawn back in a malicious grin, and Fessran, with her eyes eager, but not entirely innocent.

Ratha suddenly wished she could be down among them, waiting for someone else on the sunning rock to make the decisions and find the answers.

Her thoughts were interrupted by the sound of Thakur returning with Orange-Eyes. The Un-Named One looked guarded and wary as he followed Thakur to a place among the herders. He sought to catch Thakur's gaze, but the herding teacher, who had led him in without looking at him, turned his face away. The silvercoat lowered his head and whisked his tail away from Thakur's.

On the other side of the meeting circle, the Firekeepers stirred. Fessran rose again. "Now that the Un-Named One is among us, as he deserves to be, I may speak. I am not one to praise the clanless ones. I have seen too many of us fall to them. But, as Ratha has said, some of them hold the same light in their eyes as we do and want more than the lives of raiders and scavengers."

A hard voice broke from the growls of the herders.

"*Ptahh!* What he wants is to fill his belly with the flesh of our herdbeasts!"

Heads turned to Shoman. Fessran tried to answer, but her words were drowned in the sudden uproar. Ratha slapped the sunning rock with her paw to quiet the gathering. "Let Fessran speak." She directed a meaningful glance at Shoman.

Fessran also eyed Shoman and said, "If that's all you think he wants, why did you ask that he be brought to the meeting?"

"So that all of you may see him for what he is." Shoman's gaze darted over the group. "You, Cherfan," he said to a herder in the back, "you, who lost a lair-son to the Un-Named. You, Mondir, who buried the body of your littermate after a raid. All of you who bear scars on your coats. Look at him. Those eyes. Are they like ours? Those teeth. They could easily slash our throats." He turned back to Fessran. "You don't think of that, Firekeeper."

Fessran only yawned. "You bear no scars on your pelt," she said dryly. Some of the Firekeepers lolled their tongues in derisive grins.

Shoman's eyes blazed. "Wounds may be deep but unseen. I know my lair-father died at the jaws of the Un-Named. That is enough."

Several of the herders who were Shoman's friends flattened their ears at the Un-Named One. The silvercoat ignored them, drawing himself in and sitting stiffly.

"No, it is not enough," Fessran snapped. "What you want, Shoman, is revenge, not what is best for the rest of us. As for teeth, we all have them and we could all bite each other's throats if we were savage enough." She stamped impatiently. "You of the clan, don't you know what you saw that night of the dance-hunt? You saw someone with the strength of will to fight his fear of the Red Tongue, someone who stood his ground against my Firekeepers even when he was sick and starving."

Fessran began to circle, twitching her tail. "Yes, he wants to fill his belly. All of us do. And he will earn that right by using his courage to defend our herds."

She reared up on her hind legs, her belly fur showing golden-white in the flame's glow.

"Cherfan!" she called to him. "You lost a litterling in the Un-Named raids. What was his name?"

Cherfan reacted slowly, blinking in surprise. "He was called Shongshar."

"Good. What the Un-Named have taken, they will give back. Had Cherfan's cub lived, he would have been a brave herder and sired strong young. I have seen that this one"— she wagged her whiskers toward the silvercoat—"shows much courage in guarding the animals. As for young, we will have to wait a little while, but not too long, I think." Fessran cast a sly glance at the young females among the Firekeepers.

Trust Fessran to provide a little humor, Ratha thought, but the Firekeeper's words made her uneasy and the shadow of an old memory fell across her mind. She looked for Thakur and found him sitting stiffly. She had never seen him look so solemn.

"Shongshar is a good name," Fessran was saying. "It shouldn't be lost. Let the newcomer join and give him that name. Let the clan have a new Shongshar!"

Again there was an uproar. Ratha noticed that the silvercoat was saying the name to himself; trying it to see how it fit. Fessran, obviously enjoying the attention she was getting, swaggered over to Thakur. For an instant he didn't seem to know she was there, then he jerked his head around and faced her.

The Firekeeper's intent wasn't malicious as Shoman's had been. She did have a tendency to poke fun at those who took themselves too seriously. Ratha herself had received a few sharp digs from the claws of Fessran's wit.

"Herder, you spoke against the Un-Named One at the start of this meeting," Fessran said, still looking amused. "Why are you quiet now?" The sudden misery on his face made the Firekeeper lose her grin. Her brows drew together and she said something to Thakur in a softer tone that Ratha couldn't hear.

She caught Thakur's reply as he got to his feet.

"No, Fessran. The clan needs to hear this." He surveyed the group, looking into the eyes of all who were assembled . . . except those of the newcomer. "I wish to cast no doubt on the truth of Fessran's words. I only remind you that there are many trails to one place and each one shows us different sights. Fessran has taken you along one trail; I must show another." Thakur paused. "First I must tell you that the one who sits beside me is worthy to bear the dead cub's name. He saved a yearling from death on a herdbeast's horns. Ratha can tell you that story better than I."

"If you mean to support him," Fessran interrupted, her eyes wide, "why did you want to leave him out of the meeting?"

"I have other words besides those of praise," Thakur snapped back. "Firekeeper leader, like everyone else here, I try to make things easy for myself. What I have to say would be easier if he weren't listening to it."

Ratha caught the silvercoat peering at Thakur with

complete bewilderment in his orange eyes. One ear was cocked forward, the other back, as though he didn't know whether to be jubilant or outraged. Other clan members exchanged puzzled looks. Shoman looked completely taken aback and Ratha didn't blame him.

"We have made many mistakes about the clanless ones," said Thakur. "We thought them all witless and we found a few were not. We thought them too scattered and incapable of a major attack on the clan. We were wrong. Now we think we know enough about them to accept them into the clan. I warn you that we may be wrong again." Thakur took a breath. "Ratha, you said there have been many changes. That is so, but not all things can or should change. The old law that forbade Named from mingling with Un-Named had a reason for being. It kept the light in the cubs' eyes. If we forget it now, we risk losing what we have struggled to be."

He looked up at Ratha as he spoke, and she felt her old memory rise and wash over her like a river flood. The faces of her own cubs, with their blank animal eyes . . .

The seasons had covered that pain slowly; the days falling on it like leaves to the forest floor. Now it was back again and the pain as fresh as ever. Thakur's face seemed to change in her vision; his green eyes turning amber with a hint of bitter yellow; his scarred muzzle turning to one that was unblemished except for a broken left lower fang. Even his odor changed, becoming stronger and wilder: the scent of one who had lived alone and hunted for himself until he had taken her as his mate.

She thrust the memory away and saw the face that was really before her. *Why does Thakur have to look and smell so much like his dead brother?*

A sense of shame rose up as Bonechewer's memory receded. She had been so caught up in Fessran's idea that she had nearly forgotten the harsh lesson the past had taught her. Now she wanted to bury her head between her paws and cry aloud.

Thakur spoke again and she focused once more on his voice. "I think it is better for the Un-Named One and for ourselves that we not accept him and that he leave clan ground." For the first time since he had returned to the group, he looked the silvercoat in the face. His whiskers started to droop. "I am sorry. I wish we had thought about it sooner."

From her perch, Ratha studied the Un-Named One. The firelight played over him, making him seem to move abruptly, even though he stayed still and gazed at the clan with unreadable eyes.

Below her, arguments flew back and forth. Anger and disappointment showed on some faces, puzzlement on others. Fessran looked especially disgruntled and Ratha guessed she would not easily forgive Thakur if he destroyed her vision of a replacement for the dead Shongshar.

She caught fragments of conversations.

". . . we can let him eat from the kill, but forbid him to mate . . ."

". . . our flock is getting too large. Another herder would be helpful . . ."

". . . the way those female Firekeepers look at him? They won't be thinking of anything else once the heat has come on them . . ."

Eyes turned to her for answers, but she had none. Either choice might wreck the clan. She felt paralyzed, lost, and wished she were running free in the night, with only herself to think about. Then, out of the confusion and despair came the beginnings of an idea. It wasn't an easy one, but something told her it might work.

She jumped up and lashed her tail for silence. "I have listened to all who would speak. Now hear what I say. Fessran, you are right about our need. And Thakur, you speak wisely of the dangers. I also heard someone say we might accept the Un-Named One if he were forbidden to mate. That won't work; no one thinks of that sort of thing when the time comes.

"What I suggest is this," she continued, beginning to pace back and forth on the edge of the sunning rock. "If we allow him to take a mate from among us, he must present the cubs he sires to the rest of us so we can see whether they have the light of the Named in their eyes."

"I will be glad if they do," Thakur said. "What will happen if they don't?"

Ratha took a breath and halted her pacing. "If we judge them fit to raise in the clan, he and his mate will keep them. If not, the young ones must be taken far from clan ground and abandoned."

She crouched on the edge of the rock and stared down at the silvercoat. "You, who would be Named, do you understand?"

"Orange-eyes must show his cubs to the clan and do what the leader says."

"Yes. If you agree to that and bare your throat to the Red Tongue, I will accept you."

The meeting erupted again as those who favored and opposed the silvercoat both made their opinions known. Triumphant roars and angry hisses filled the air. The emotions battered at Ratha, throwing her back. She leaped up, adding her voice to the tumult. "Be silent, all of you! The decision is mine and I have made it."

The meeting quieted, but an undercurrent of muttering continued. She leaped down and stood before the gathering. "Are you ready?" Ratha asked the Un-Named One. "Then come to the sunning rock."

She ordered two torchbearers to stand on either side while Fessran lighted another brand and brought it to her. Before she took it between her jaws she lifted her muzzle. "Crouch and bare your throat." A sudden fear jumped in his eyes and she knew he remembered the dance-hunt. The clan watched, waiting. If his will failed him now, both he and she would lose.

She lifted the torch high. He took his place as she bid and lifted his chin, turning his head so that she could see the pulse beat in his throat beneath the fur.

"Now to them," she said, around the branch in her teeth. Obediently he turned and bared his throat to the clan. The sight of his submission seemed to calm the group. He prolonged his awkward crouch with his head strained up until Ratha told him to rise. She flung her torch back into the fire.

"Stand before the clan . . . Shongshar!" she cried. "Let the Named greet their new lair-brother."

At first the newly named Shongshar stood alone, but gradually the clanfolk began to surround him, touching noses and exchanging cheek rubs. When Fessran and the Firekeepers joined in, things became more enthusiastic. Their friendly assault nearly knocked Shongshar over, but Ratha saw that he bore it in good humor, especially since they all left their torches behind.

The herders were less excited, but even Shoman grudgingly brushed whiskers. Thakur gave his pupil a formal nose-touch and came to sit by Ratha. Neither one of them spoke as they watched the crowd of well-wishers wash over and around Shongshar.

She couldn't help feeling a small glow of pride.

"You're making a mistake," said Thakur softly, his whiskers in her ear.

"*Arr,* don't spoil it, Thakur."

"All right. I am happy for him, but I hope you know the trail you're running."

"I have to. There is no other."

He fell silent again. She felt deflated and couldn't help but remember her uncertainty about the newcomer and the subtle defiance she had once sensed in him. Surely she was wrong about that . . . or was she?

Suddenly, she was disgusted by her own ambivalence and told herself to stop fretting. *I've done what is best for us. I can't ask myself for more. Only the passing days will tell me whether I was right. I won't think about it any more. I don't need to hunt trouble.*

CHAPTER 6

THAKUR SAT in the dry leaves underneath the oak and watched the yearlings manage the dapple-backs and three-horns by themselves. He hoped his training had prepared the young herders well enough for the work ahead of them. It was fall now, and the clan's mating season had begun. During this time, the yearlings took charge of the animals, for the cubs had not reached the age to heed the meaning of new scents carried across the meadow on the autumn wind.

Thakur smelled the odors of females in heat. He prickled and quivered as each smell tantalized his nose. He jerked his tail restlessly, wishing the mating season hadn't come so soon.

He would leave clan ground, he promised himself. His work preparing the youthful herders was done. Now he and the other clan adults would have to trust the skill and courage of the youngsters. Judging from the smells and the yowling courtship songs that filled the air, he doubted that any of the other clan members were thinking about the herd. Perhaps the cries of the courting males would have irritated him less if he hadn't recognized Shongshar's voice among them.

Thakur had hoped that the silvercoat's youth would delay his mating for a year, postponing difficulties that might arise over the cubs he would sire. But Shongshar was older than he looked, and his rapid development into a fully mature male suprised many in the clan. A few days earlier, he had begun courting the young Firekeeper Bira, edging out Cherfan, who was also seeking her attention. The herder retreated with good grace, but admitted to Thakur that he had underestimated Shongshar as a rival. "That young rake has a louder voice than I do, if you can believe it," Cherfan had said, lolling his tongue in a rueful grimace.

Thakur tried to tell himself that his reaction to Shongshar's success was only jealousy, but there was a part of his mind that refused to accept such an easy answer. He had spoken to Shongshar about the possible consequences of his mating and the silvercoat's answers had disturbed him.

"Shongshar, have you thought about Ratha's words to you when you joined the clan?" Thakur had asked him one rainy evening not long after the ceremony that made him one of the Named. He remembered how the silvercoat turned his head, blinking as rain dripped from his eyebrow whiskers onto his nose. "She make me say when I mate and cubs are born I must bring them before her. Only if they have light in their eyes can my mate and me raise them."

"And if your cubs don't have the light of the Named in their eyes, they must be left to die. Have you thought about that?" Thakur persisted.

"I think it will be harder for female I mate with than for me," Shongshar answered. "I won't bear the cubs and nurse them. If eyes are empty, cubs will mean little to me."

"You wouldn't regret having to give them up?"

"No, herding teacher. Why you ask this?" Shongshar stopped, then cocked his head at Thakur.

"You seem to like being with the litterlings. I've seen you working with them. You almost got into a fight with Shoman when he bullied Bundi."

"Is that bad?"

"No," Thakur answered, "but it isn't something I expected from you. Are you sure your fondness for the litterlings might not make you want to keep the cubs you sire?"

Shongshar looked thoughtful. "Herding teacher, not to worry. There is big difference between litterlings that are stupid as herdbeasts and those whose eyes shine bright. Even if they are mine."

I wonder, thought Thakur.

"It won't be hard for me. Don't worry," said Shongshar lightly, and he had walked away, leaving the herding teacher full of doubt.

More yowls from the forest interrupted Thakur's thoughts. He got up and shook the leaf litter from his fur. The yearlings were busy with the herd and no one was watching him. He should go.

He left the oak and paced away as a deep roar answered one of the calls. *What a fuss everybody made about the mating season!* he thought crossly. *Why couldn't one choose not to be involved without being thought peculiar?* He had never been very successful with the females; they drove him off in favor of stronger, louder or more odoriferous males. Even when Ratha's leadership had raised his status from one who was barely tolerated to one who was eagerly accepted and respected, habit had still made him shy away.

Habit and something else, he admitted to himself as he jogged across the meadow. He, too, could share in the joys that this time brought if it weren't for the uncertainty of his half Un-Named parentage. There was a small chance that cubs he sired would bear the gift of the Named, but he knew that his brother Bonechewer's mating with Ratha had produced witless young. Any cubs that Thakur sired were likely to turn out the same.

If he went to her now, as her smell, wafting on the breeze, tempted him to do, she would accept him eagerly without thinking of the consequences. In that she would be like any Named female caught in the fever of her heat. Yet if she did, and her cubs were born as he feared, he would have wounded her in a way that might never heal.

He knew that she took a partner each season, but the male left only a lingering odor on her fur, for there were

never any cubs. He had once asked Ratha if she understood why. He never asked her again, however, for the
look of pain on her face had tightened his own throat as
she answered. "I mated after Bonechewer and I lost the
cubs. Again I took a mate, but my belly never swelled.
Why, I don't know. Somehow my body won't let me bear
another litter. Perhaps I can't forget what happened to
the first."

"Your cubs wouldn't be witless this time," Thakur had
said. "Not if you take a clan male. Why don't you try
again?"

"I will. I can't help but try again. When the heat draws
me I don't think of such things, but afterward . . ."

There would be nothing to regret. Still, he would not
risk siring empty-eyed cubs on her. It was better that he
stay away and so he had done each year, wandering the
forests and grasslands beyond clan territory. This self-
imposed exile was a lonely and bitter time for him. Without a companion, the journey became a weary one, and
his mind often strayed back to those he had left behind.
Had Shongshar not reached adulthood this season, he
might have joined Thakur on the trail, but now he was
back there in the midst of all the growls and tail-wavings.
Thakur would go alone, returning only when his belly
called him, to eat of the yearling herders' cull and slip
away again before he could be drawn into the fever of
courtship.

With these thoughts burdening his mind, Thakur jogged
heavily toward the stream that marked the edge of clan
territory. It was just beginning to swell with the first
winter rains. The water buffeted his legs as he waded in
the shallows. It was only deep enough to splash his belly,
but if more rain came he might have to swim back across.

That thought and his wet paws did nothing to ease his temper. Mournful cries in the sky made him lift his head to see birds circling high over the tree-covered hills in the direction he was going. The cries made him think of hooked beaks and quick, sharp talons; he wondered what carrion they had found.

The wind that stole the warmth from the wet fur on his belly seemed to chill his mind as well. A good run would warm him up and stretch his muscles, he decided.

On the other side of the creek, Thakur swung into a fluid canter, watching the foliage race past as a blur on either side of him. He was proud of his speed and often ran for the sheer joy of feeling the ground slip away beneath his flying paws. He was galloping down a long grade on a deer trail beneath overhanging boughs when something darted onto the path between his legs.

One of his front paws struck it. There was a sharp screech as the object flew into the air. Whirling his tail to keep his balance, Thakur bounced to a stop, then retraced his steps to see what had tripped him.

The object moved slowly and unevenly. The culprit was a small furball dragging itself crabwise through the fallen leaves. It was the same size as a nursing cub, although not at all the same shape. He cocked his head, torn between caution and curiosity. Carefully he sidled up to it and reached out with an inquisitive paw. The creature showed tiny teeth and a pink tongue. It tried to hitch itself across the trail again but soon stopped. One rear leg was limp and dragging.

Thakur circled the animal as it squatted in the trail, following him with frightened eyes. It had a short banded muzzle, paws that bore nails instead of claws and a ringed furry tail. It was one of the tree-dwellers who had often pestered him when he tried to nap in the shade of their trees.

Here was a chance for revenge, if he wanted it, or an opportunity to find out how these creatures might taste. At least it would extend his time away from the clan by sating his belly a little.

The young treeling hunched itself in the dead leaves, giving him quick nervous glances. He could see its small sides heave and the way its racing heartbeat rocked it. He smelled the fear that seeped from the small animal. Sensing that it was helpless, the creature curled its tail around itself and clung to it as if clinging to its mother. It began to stroke and pick nervously at the fur, never taking its eyes from him.

His attention was oddly drawn to the movements of the creature's paws. As he watched the small fingers twine in the hair, he felt something like an itch in his mind, a thought that almost came forward but then disappeared.

Thakur nosed the treeling. It tried to curl up into a ball, but the injured leg got in the way. He turned the creature over with his paw, his belly still warring with the strange itch in his mind.

The treeling, after sitting rigidly for a long time, made a sudden scramble for safety. Thakur stepped firmly on its tail. It twisted back and tried to bite his foot. He fastened his jaws loosely around its neck and picked it up. The animal went limp, but Thakur could feel its heart beating against his lips. For a moment, he felt ridiculous and his instinct was to snap it up into his mouth or fling it into the bushes with a sharp toss of his head.

I'm taking it with me, he decided at last. *If it dies, I'll eat it and if it doesn't . . . well, it might be amusing.*

For the rest of the day he carried the treeling, grateful

that no one of the clan was there to see him or to ask why. He shifted his grip from its neck to its scruff, which seemed to make it a little less frightened. When at last he let the creature down, it shook its soaked fur, spraying him with his own saliva.

He washed his face, made a comfortable nest and settled into it, then reached out a paw for the treeling. The animal tried to hitch itself away, but he swept it up, dragged it into the nest and crossed his paws over it. It made one little peep of protest and was still.

The next morning, Thakur was mildly surprised to find the treeling still alive and sleeping under his paw. As soon as he moved, it woke, hissed and nipped his pad. Despite its injured leg, the creature was quite lively, and it was all he could do to keep it from escaping through the grass, or fastening its small teeth in him. At last he managed to grab the animal by the scruff and shake it a few times to reduce it to a state of grudging acceptance.

At midday, Thakur stopped beside a little brook trickling between the gnarled roots of two fire-scarred pines. He was grateful to come into the shade, for the autumn sun on his back had warmed him during the journey and, with the treeling in his mouth, he couldn't pant to cool himself off.

He put his soggy passenger down and dipped his muzzle in the stream, washing away the taste of treeling fur. With one paw on the animal's tail, he surveyed the grove into which he'd come. The place felt peaceful and quiet without being gloomy. He could stay here awhile, perhaps dig a shallow den near the stream. First, though, he'd have to figure out what to do with his treeling.

Thakur found a soft spot under a young fir and, holding the treeling in his mouth, started scraping pine needles and litter away. Soon he had excavated a deep treeling refuge in the red clay beneath the tree. He lowered the animal gently into the hole, arranged branches and needles over it, then piled dirt on the covering before the creature could claw its way out. He stamped the soil down and waited to see if the creature would unbury itself. When he saw no sign that it was escaping, he turned to the task of digging himself a temporary den and forgot about the treeling.

In the morning, he slept late, enjoying his solitude. Here there were no tail-waving females or yowling males. No one of the clan was there to press him with their needs or fears. He heard only the quiet trickle of the brook and felt the pine-scented breeze teasing his whiskers. Until he remembered the treeling.

Thakur jumped up and ran to the little fir, only to find that he had packed the dirt down harder than he'd thought. It took determined digging to reopen the burrow. When at last he broke through, he almost dug the treeling up along with the dirt. The little creature made no attempt to escape, for it was nearly suffocated.

He pawed some clay from the brindled pelt. The treeling closed its eyes and made no protest. At first he felt relieved and then alarmed. Its passivity was probably due to hunger, he thought, and he decided he'd better feed it. But what would it eat? Well, if treelings lived in trees, they probably ate leaves, he concluded, and went off to find some.

He brought one type of leaf after another, without success. The treeling would eat none of them. At last, by accident he brought a branch that had several beetles on it. When he placed his offering outside the treeling's hole, it poked its head out, spied a bug, snatched it up and crammed the morsel into its mouth. It continued to pick insects off the branch until all of them were gone. It looked up at Thakur with inquisitive eyes, cocked its head slightly and said *"Aree?"*

Later that morning found Thakur in a nearby stretch of grassland, hunting grasshoppers. He had been quite adept at this when he was a cub, although now he found lack of practice had robbed him of some skill. Finally he managed to catch one in his mouth and carry it back to the treeling, feeling the struggling insect kicking his tongue. He spat it out in front of the treeling's burrow. A small arm emerged, caught the insect by the leg and dragged it inside. Thakur could hear more crunching sounds.

After the grasshopper hunt, Thakur stretched out for a nap in the autumn sun. He was almost asleep when he felt something climb up his back and nestle in the fur on his flank. Startled, he shook the treeling off and nosed it back into the burrow. He returned to his nap.

When he woke, he found that the treeling had climbed up on him again and was clinging to his pelt. He craned his head back, seized the creature by the scruff and pulled, but it had woven fingers and toes into his fur. Realizing that he would pull the treeling apart before he got it off, he sighed and let it stay.

After a while, he found he enjoyed having the treeling on his back. It murmured contentedly as he jogged along and made small wordless comments whenever anything happened. At first Thakur was afraid he might lose his new companion and he chose his way carefully, avoiding low branches, lest his passenger be swept off or scramble into the trees beyond his reach. He made wide detours and looked over his shoulder at every step to assure himself that the creature was still there. The treeling stared back at him, the expression on its short-muzzled face saying, "I'm still here. What are you so worried about?"

Soon Thakur ceased worrying about losing the animal. It seemed to like riding on him and sleeping in his fur at night. During the following days, he roamed far from the grove, carrying the treeling with him and feeding it on beetles and the big grasshoppers that lived in the nearby meadowlands.

He doubted that this was the food the creature had been accustomed to, but it seemed to be flourishing on its new diet. Thakur also ate a few of the insects himself, to ward off the hunger that threatened to drive him back to the clan. Eventually, he knew, he would have to go, and what was he going to do with the treeling then?

Well, it was the mating season. None of the adults in the clan would pay any attention to him. He would have to show himself to the yearlings who were guarding the herd and the fires; otherwise he might be attacked as an enemy by the over-eager youngsters. He would receive some curious stares from his pupils, but his previous authority over them would keep them from asking too many questions or trying to eat his new friend.

Friend? He was startled by the thought. Never had he supposed he could think about any other kind of animal as more than food, yet he had to admit that the treeling's presence often brought him a quiet sort of contentment.

Thakur couldn't help grinning as he ambled along with the creature on his back. "You funny little treeling-cub," he said, glancing over his shoulder at it. "Sometimes I wonder if you know what I'm thinking. Perhaps I should give you a name if I'm going to talk to you as I talk to the ones in the clan."

The treeling looked at him with wide solemn eyes. *"Aree,"* it said, as if it were agreeing with him.

"I probably shouldn't. You don't know what a name means. It means you know what you are. Treeling-cub, do you know what you are?"

It cocked its head at him.

"I suppose it doesn't matter. I think you're a 'he' and I have to call you something besides 'treeling.' What should I call you? Fur-Puller? Bug-Cruncher?"

"Aree!"

"Well, all right. Since that's the only word you know, I'll call you Aree."

A little later the same day, Thakur was passing under a curtain of leaves when the treeling jumped from his back into the branches. By the time Thakur realized that Aree was gone, he had climbed beyond sight. The tree was too slight for Thakur to climb any farther than to the first crotch and there he perched, looking anxiously up into the branches and yowling helplessly, hoping Aree would come back.

Soon there was a rustle and Aree plopped down on him, making him lose his balance and topple out of the tree. A wild swing of his tail enabled him to land on his feet with the treeling still attached. When he peered back over his shoulder, he noticed that Aree was carrying something smooth and round. He had seen similar objects hanging on some trees, but since he never ate any part of a tree, he never paid attention to these things unless he stepped on one that was rotten.

Aree was fascinated. The treeling turned his prize over in his paws, looking at it and smelling it. The little creature had to stretch his jaws wide before he was able to bite into the skin, but once he did, he began munching away as if he had never tasted anything so delicious in his short life.

The fruit the treeling picked was overripe and the syrupy juice dribbled onto Thakur's back. It ran down his side and matted his fur, making him itch. Irritated, he nudged Aree aside and cleaned his coat, but as fast as he licked himself, the treeling dribbled more juice on him.

The taste of the stuff was sweet and the only sweet flavor Thakur knew was the taste of spoiled meat. That was enough to make him stop licking. He tried to ignore the smears on his coat, but as the afternoon passed, the sun warmed his back, turning the dribbles into sticky patches and dry, crusty spots. Once Aree had discovered this new treat, he sought more and couldn't be persuaded to dismount while eating. Thakur's back and neck fur were soon stiff with dried dribbles and his skin itched unbearably.

There were a few flies still left from summer and they all began to swarm around him. The treeling, unconcerned, continued to stuff himself. Unable to stand the torment any longer, Thakur finally dislodged Aree by threatening to roll over on him. While the treeling sulked, he licked his back and sides, digging out sticky mats of hair in which entrapped flies buzzed angrily.

Sometimes the treeling picked more than he could eat and became fussy, taking one bite and throwing the rest away. Thakur often retrieved the discards, licking the juice from them. The first time he tried to eat one, he gagged on the pulpy texture. Once he had grown used to that, he tried to crack the pit as he would a bone. He found no marrow inside, only evil-tasting seeds. He spat everything out and opened his mouth wide, drooling saliva on the ground. He ran for the stream, almost leaving Aree behind, and lapped until the bitter taste was gone.

Thakur also discovered an interesting property of this new food. Many of the fruits still hanging had begun to ferment; eating those made his tongue tingle. Afterwards he felt warm and happy, often chasing his tail and bouncing around like a cub. Eating too many made him clumsy, and he couldn't keep his paws from sliding out from under him. His head also ached a little. The treeling chirped happily and wobbled on his back.

The treeling once became so drunk that he fell out of a tree. A clump of ferns cushioned his landing, but he couldn't ride without toppling off. Thakur had to carry Aree back to the den in his mouth. Thakur suffered also from the treeling's overindulgence, for he had been eating Aree's leavings. He was stricken with a severe digestive upset that made him forget the mild pain in his head. The two spent the rest of the day in the makeshift den, sleeping much of the time and ill-tempered when they were awake. As he lay groaning, Thakur swore he would never touch his tongue to the cursed stuff again.

Aree recovered first, but the illness laid Thakur low for several days. During that time Aree stayed with him, gently grooming his fur or snuggling against him, making soft reassuring sounds. At last his stomach started to behave itself again and he was able to stagger out of the den, shaky and thin.

He knew he needed meat and he would have to return to the clan for it. He guessed the mating season was almost over, judging by how long he'd been away. Of course now he must worry about what to do with his treeling, but at least he'd have some time to think about it on the trail.

CHAPTER 7

THAKUR FELT the treeling dig his paws deeper into his fur and crouch low on his back. He peered through the gray drizzle that sifted between the trees and looked toward the meadow where the herd grazed. Smoke billowed above the grass and he saw the amber flicker of fire. The treeling shook himself and fluffed his fur. Thakur could feel how uneasy Aree was by the way he shivered and clung. A gust of wind blew the smoke toward them. The herding teacher had almost forgotten how smoke stung his nose. He sneezed and glanced at Aree as the treeling drew back his whiskers and rubbed his muzzle with the back of his paw.

Thakur circled along the edge of the meadow and approached upwind of the guard-fire, allowing his scent to drift ahead of him to announce his presence to the young Firekeeper. The yearling might be nervous, and a mistaken attack could frighten Aree away. Soon Thakur could see the ring of guard flames that surrounded the clan's animals.

He jogged toward a point midway between the closest outlying guard-fires. A Firekeeper came out to meet him. At the sight of Thakur, the youngster's tail went up and a look of relief came over his face. Thakur guessed that he was anxious for the clan adults to return from mating and take over their duties once again.

"Welcome back, herding teacher!" the Firekeeper called. He stopped, stared and cocked his head. Thakur knew the yearling had seen something odd about him, but he wasn't about to stop to answer questions. He quickened his pace.

As he crossed the meadow, he glanced toward the oak where several clan members had taken shelter from the misty rain. Among them he saw the gleam of a silver pelt. He hadn't thought of Shongshar in a while. Having Aree as a companion had distracted him from his old doubts, but now they came back in a rush. Shongshar's head lifted and he trotted out to meet Thakur.

Thakur felt ashamed of his worries. Shongshar had already proven himself a worthy and valued member of the group, the herding teacher reminded himself. It seemed that only he, Thakur, continued to doubt him. And that doubt was not based on Shongshar's character but on the things he couldn't control, such as the length of his fangs, the manner of his bite and the uncertainty of his parentage. Was it really fair to hold such things against him?

As Shongshar approached, Thakur could see that he had grown heavier; the powerful muscling in his shoulders and neck was even more evident. Now he was almost full-grown, and there was an air of maturity and a new sense of assurance about him. When the silvercoat drew closer, Thakur could see why. Shongshar's muzzle was marked with claw scratches. The herding teacher had seen those marks on other young males after the mating season. The older males had enough experience to jump away before the female could claw them, but younger ones often caught their partner's sudden change of mood too late to prevent a strike across the face.

For many of the young males, this was a badge of

maturity and they wore their wounds proudly, as Shong-shar did now. He slowed from a jog into an easy walk, his tail swinging. Again Thakur felt Aree tense as Shongshar's scent reached them. The silvercoat, however, seemed to know the need to keep his distance.

"Herding teacher, if you're hungry, there is a fresh kill," said Shongshar at last, after eyeing the treeling. "You are among the first to return, and the yearlings have left plenty."

His words reminded Thakur that his stomach hadn't been filled with fresh meat in many days. He was seized by a strong hunger that cramped his belly and made him weak.

"Over here, herding teacher." Shongshar led the way under the oak. At the sight of the kill, Thakur forgot everything else and ate until the pangs in his stomach had eased. When he felt sated, he scrubbed his muzzle and washed behind his ears, bumping the treeling with his forepaw.

He yawned, feeling the satisfying weight of a full belly. "Ah, that is so much better!" he said, stretching out and not minding the damp grass.

Shongshar ate a few bites and then washed himself as Thakur had done, stopping now and then to study the treeling. "What does it eat?" he asked.

"Bugs. And those soft things that hang on trees."

Shongshar wrinkled his nose. "Oh." He sat up, his nose in the air and then listened attentively. "I think some of the others are coming."

Unwillingly, Thakur got up. All he wanted was to lie down and digest his dinner, but he had to do something with Aree before the other clanfolk arrived.

They got there much sooner than he expected. He had

only reached the path that led to the dens when a whole group of long-absent clan members spilled out of the underbrush and greeted him with enthusiastic rubs and nuzzles. With a terrified squeal, Aree dived underneath him and clung to the long fur on his belly. Everyone retreated in surprise and Thakur was able to sort them all out. He saw Shoman, Cherfan and Fessran on one side of him, Ratha and Bira on the other. They looked tired and thin, but happy. They also looked and smelled hungry.

Their voices tumbled together in his ears.

"Is that a tree-creature, Thakur?"

"Where did you get it?"

"Are you going to eat it?"

"I've never had one of those before. Can I have a taste?"

"It smells good. Come on, aren't you going to share?"

Thakur looked frantically for a way out of the ring of hungry friends. He could feel Aree trembling and pulling his belly fur so hard that it hurt. They all crowded around him again, except for the clan leader, who stood back watching, with an annoying look of amusement on her face.

"Ratha!" Thakur bellowed, trying to guard Aree from inquisitive muzzles and paws.

She waded in among the group, butting, shoving and dealing out cuffs to those who didn't get out of her way. "All right, leave Thakur alone, you greedy bunch. I smell a kill over by the oak; the yearlings are welcoming us back."

Cherfan lifted his head and tail. His eyes brightened and he galloped away, followed by Shoman, Fessran and Bira.

"Leave enough for me!" Ratha roared after them before she turned back to Thakur.

Aree had stopped shaking, but he still clung tightly to Thakur's underside. Ratha paced around the herding teacher, trying to peek under his belly at the treeling. He could hear her stomach growl, and he wasn't sure whether her interest was just curiosity.

"Are you really going to keep this creature?" she asked at last.

"Shouldn't I?"

"Well, I don't know. No one in the clan has ever kept one. I'm not sure why anyone would want to. Are you waiting for it to grow fatter so it will make more of a mouthful?"

"The meat is over there," Thakur said icily, flicking his whiskers in the direction of the old oak. "If you can't think of anything except your belly, go and eat."

Ratha reassured him that she wouldn't eat his treeling but there was still a spark of mischief in her eyes. She admitted one could keep a creature for reasons other than eating it. After all, she had tamed and kept the Red Tongue.

"I don't think this treeling is quite the same as the creature I brought to the clan," she said critically as Aree grew bold enough to leave his refuge under Thakur's belly and clamber up onto his back. With a suspicious look at her, the treeling began grooming himself again; once he had finished, he started to part Thakur's fur, sifting through his pelt.

Ratha grimaced. "*Yarr!* He's putting his paws into your coat. Doesn't that feel terrible?"

"At first it did, but now I don't mind," Thakur answered. Ratha sat down and scratched herself briefly.

"What's he doing?" She stared harder at the treeling.

"Aree is eating my ticks. He's cleaned me off pretty

well and I don't have many fleas either. You probably have more than I do now."

"I probably do. When the fleabane plant dies in the winter, we scratch until spring." Ratha added the action to the word. When she stood up again, Thakur bumped up against her and tried to nudge the treeling onto her back.

"Oh no." She sidled away. "I don't want that thing pawing through my fur."

"Are you afraid of a treeling after you've tamed the Red Tongue?" Thakur lolled his tongue at her.

"Of course not!" Ratha's whiskers bristled.

"You want to get rid of all those itchy fleas, don't you?"

"I don't think he will climb on me," Ratha said, but Thakur could see her resistance was weakening.

"He will if you don't try to eat him."

Still looking doubtful, Ratha edged against Thakur. He nosed the reluctant treeling off his back. Aree hissed at him and gave his whiskers a pull before he scrambled onto her and began to groom her ruff. Aree buried his muzzle in her pelt and bit at something. Alarmed, Thakur tried to take the treeling off, unsure whether he was trying to bite Ratha or something in her fur.

"No, leave him," she said suddenly. She winced, then looked relieved. "Ooh, that hurt. Your treeling just pulled out the wretched tick I've been carrying around for days. I couldn't reach it with my teeth. What a relief!"

She let the treeling clean the rest of her back. When Aree was done, he jumped back onto Thakur and nestled between his shoulders, murmuring softly.

"Well?" Thakur looked at Ratha.

"Your creature felt like all the fleas in the forest were on my back, but I am glad to be rid of that tick." Ratha shook herself. "Keep your treeling, then. I will tell the others not to eat the creature. He isn't like the Red Tongue, but he seems to be useful. Will he groom others in the clan besides you and me?"

"If they are gentle and don't frighten him."

"What are you going to do with him now?" she asked.

"Take him to my den. I think he wants to sleep."

Ratha gave the treeling one more look. "I'm going to ask the yearlings if anything happened while I was gone," she said and jogged away, swinging her tail. Thakur gazed after her, then turned up the path that led to his den. With his full stomach, he agreed with the treeling that a nap would be a good idea.

CHAPTER 8

MOST OF THE MATED females became pregnant, carrying their cubs through the winter and giving birth in early spring. When the rainy season ended, the clan mothers brought their litterlings from the birth-dens to a secluded place amid an outcropping of stone. In this sheltered nursery, guarded by one or two females, the small cubs could sleep in the sun or crawl about on unsteady legs.

The nursery would have been too hot at midday if it hadn't been for the shade of a sapling that leaned over the rocks. A gap in the lichen-dotted stones allowed a light breeze to cool the litterlings, but the nursery's shelter kept out the chill of the early spring wind.

Ratha lay, half-asleep, with a heap of dozing cubs warming her belly. As in previous years, she had had no cubs of her own; she took nursery duty to allow the mothers a rest. She opened one eye and watched the sapling's new leaves flutter in the breeze.

A fuzzy, chubby body blocked her view and little paws stepped on her face. The cub was too tiny to hurt her and she let him clamber across her muzzle, only objecting when he stopped halfway to chew on her whiskers. With a grunt, she shook him off, caught him by the scruff and swung him into the pile of his fellows who were still asleep.

"Hmph. Your mother had better teach you that my whiskers aren't blades of grass, even though they may look that way when I'm lying down," she grumbled, giving him a nudge with her nose.

She lay back to enjoy the quiet, but soon other litterlings woke and began climbing all over her, butting her with their heads and digging in the fur of her belly to find her nipples. They would have to stay hungry until one of the mothers came to feed them, she thought, regretting she had no milk.

"Sleep until Fessran comes and she will feed you," she said.

Ratha flicked her tail away from a cub that had started gnawing on it, surprised that such tiny teeth could be so sharp. She tried to nap again, but the litterlings wouldn't leave her alone. She was starting to lose some of her patience when Fessran slithered through the opening in the rocks and flopped down to feed the hungry young. There were tiny squeals and growls as the small cubs fought for places at her teats. Ratha sat and watched, smelling the rich scent of flowing milk as the cubs nursed.

"Well, has our clan leader had enough of tending nurslings?" Fessran teased.

"They don't squabble as much as the grown cubs I have to look after," Ratha said.

Fessran grunted. "Give them time. They will. Especially mine." She leaned over to nudge her little male and left a sooty smudge on him. "The black stuff won't hurt," said Fessran. "It's just another spot. I'll clean him up when I'm through nursing the rest."

"Being a Firekeeper's cub may have its problems," Ratha teased. "If he keeps gaining spots, how will he ever lose them as he should when he grows up?"

Fessran yawned. "Speaking of Firekeepers' cubs, has Bira brought hers out yet?"

"No. She had a late litter. They're still too young."

"*Ptahh!* She had them not long after I had mine. She's just afraid that hers aren't going to be the best. They're not, of course, but I'm sure they'll be acceptable. I think you should have a talk with her. She should be helping the rest of us mothers with the nursery."

"She's young; this is her first litter," Ratha protested. "I don't want to bother her yet. But I am curious about Shongshar. Does he take an interest in the litter?"

"Yes. He is more concerned with his cubs than any male I've known."

"He seems to be good with youngsters," Ratha said reflectively, getting up. The prospect of Shongshar having a strong attachment to his cubs made her uneasy, but she did not voice her concerns to the Firekeeper. Instead, she asked, "Is Shongshar as good a Firekeeper as you had hoped he'd be? I know the guard-fires have stayed strong and we haven't recently lost any animals to raiders."

Fessran's eyes lit with pride as she answered, "Shongshar is as good as I'd hoped and even better. Not only is he brave and quick, but he sets a good example for the younger Firekeepers and encourages them to work harder."

"Good." Ratha let her uneasiness fade.

The cubs who hadn't found a place to nurse crawled all over Fessran, their mewing shrill and insistent.

"Is someone coming to help you feed the litterlings?" Ratha asked.

"Drani is coming and her teats are full." Fessran grimaced and shoved a cub away from her belly. "Ouch, you little son of a mare! You're supposed to suck, not chew."

With that, Ratha took her leave.

During the next few days, she found herself watching both Shongshar and Bira. Shongshar was immensely proud of his new offspring and it showed in every step he took. Bira, however, seemed subdued. She was pleased at having her first cubs. But the happiness Ratha saw in the eyes of other mothers was marred in hers by uncertainty. Bira still did not bring her litterlings to the nursery and Ratha decided, reluctantly, that it was time to speak to her about it.

It was just after sunset and she was resting in her den trying to think of the best way to approach the young mother about her secrecy. She heard the tread of someone approaching and smelled Fessran. She raised her head, catching the sharp scent of anger in the Firekeeper's odor.

"What is it?" she asked as Fessran came to the mouth of the den, her tail wagging and her fur bristling.

"That little idiot Bira!" Fessran hissed. "She's abandoned her cubs. Shongshar came to me when he found them cold and hungry. She must have gone mad. I've never heard of anyone doing such a thing."

A prickling apprehension began to creep over Ratha. "Is Shongshar with you?"

"No. He's with the cubs, trying to keep them warm. I'll go to Bira's den and nurse them if you'll try to find her."

Ratha hesitated. Invading a new mother's lair was not something that clan females usually did. Each of them knew how fiercely they guarded their own privacy and the right to decide whether they would show their cubs. Only the clan leader could violate that privacy and only when there was need. Fessran hadn't said it directly, but Ratha knew she was asking for permission to enter Bira's den.

"All right. Go feed them." Ratha crawled out of the den and shook herself, trying to get rid of the cold chill that seemed to crawl through her fur. It was a worry she had long suppressed and had almost forgotten about. Now it came back in Thakur's words and his voice.

"No," she growled to herself. Fessran gave her a puzzled look.

"Nothing. Go on. I'll find Bira. Where did you see her last?"

"At one of the guard-fires around the meadow. Her partner left, but she may have stayed," Fessran said and bounded away.

Ratha took the trail that led to the meadow. Bira's scent was present, but faint, telling Ratha that the Firekeeper had gone to the meadow but had not returned. When Ratha arrived, she looked into the night, narrowing her eyes so she could see farther. At the most distant flame she made out the form of a single fire-tender.

As Ratha neared the fire, Bira charged out, her ears flattened and her teeth bared. "Go away! I told everyone I don't need any help."

Ratha held her ground. Bira's pace slowed and her lashing tail went stiff. "I appreciate your diligence, Fire-keeper," Ratha said dryly. "But there are others who are waiting to serve their turn at duty."

Bira's eyes widened in dismay. "Clan leader! I didn't mean . . ."

"I know you didn't," Ratha said, trying to make her voice sound kind. "Come back to the fire and tell me why you abandoned your cubs."

Bira followed her back to the circle of warm light thrown by the guard-fire. Ratha saw that Bira's red-brown coat was rough and her tail ungroomed and matted. The young mother's nipples bulged with too much milk and she admitted that they hurt.

"Why don't you go and feed your litterlings?" Ratha asked again. Bira flinched and ducked her head, saying nothing.

"Is there something the matter with them?"

Bira trembled and then gave a little jerk as if she wanted to jump up and flee. She turned her head away and gazed with longing into the night. This was not like Bira at all, Ratha thought. She had always been calm and level-headed, even as a cub. Her only fault was vanity; she was overly proud of her long bushy tail. That she had ceased to groom herself told how troubled she was.

As Ratha watched her, she grew more certain that she knew the cause of Bira's distress.

"Bira," she said softly. "Are you afraid your cubs have no light in their eyes?"

The young mother shuddered and suddenly the words

burst out of her. "Shongshar thinks there's nothing wrong with them, but he doesn't know. I'm the one who sees the lack of something in their eyes. I'm the one who tries to get them to say their first word, afraid that they will never speak . . ."

"Bira, it's too early to tell," Ratha said, trying to make herself believe her own words. "Have any of the cubs in other litters begun to talk?"

"No . . . but they try. Fessran said that her little female is starting to imitate her and makes noises that are almost words."

"*Ptahh!* Fessran brags about her young. All the mothers do," Ratha said, trying to comfort her. "And you should know better than to listen to them."

But Bira didn't seem convinced. "No," she said stubbornly, looking at the ground. "There is something wrong. Maybe I carried them too long or my milk is bad."

"There's nothing wrong with your milk," Ratha insisted. Bira said nothing. She sat and shivered even in the warmth of the fire. For a long time she stared at nothing.

"Fessran asked to nurse your cubs," Ratha said at last. "I told her to feed them. I can't let litterlings starve just because you think there is something wrong with them. We need every cub we can raise. I want you to take them back and care for them until we know if they can be named. Will you go and nurse them?"

Bira shut her eyes. "No, clan leader."

Ratha sighed. "Well, I can't drag you to your den and force you to nurse. Since Fessran is willing to feed your young, would you be willing to care for hers?"

"If my milk made my litterlings sick, wouldn't it hurt hers?" Bira asked.

"I don't think so," said Ratha patiently.

"I'm sorry. I didn't mean to cause all this trouble . . . yes, I will feed Fessran's cubs."

Bira gave the guard-fire some more wood and then followed Ratha back across the meadow. The clan leader waved her tail at two other Firekeepers, who promptly took Bira's place.

The young mother wasn't sure that Fessran's cubs would accept her, but soon Bira was lying on her side in the maternal lair with three cubs sucking and kneading her belly. Once she had been made comfortable, Ratha went to the other den to tell Fessran that her young were being cared for. Then she returned to her own den and fell into an uneasy sleep.

The next morning Ratha came by to see how Bira's cubs were faring. When she arrived at the den, Fessran had finished feeding them and was gone. Shongshar was taking them out of the den to play. This was the first time she had seen his young in full daylight and she studied the cubs carefully.

Even though his litterlings were slightly younger than most of the clan cubs, they seemed older. They were larger, stronger and steadier on their legs than cubs in other litters. Although their heads had the same round baby form as other cubs', there was a subtle hint that they would develop the same arched skull as their father. The color of the fur between their spots was a fawn so light it looked ashy, with touches of silver-gray. Their infant chubbiness couldn't quite hide the heavier forequarters and longer forelegs. Their paws were large, showing that they would someday equal their father in size. The smell on them was more Shongshar's than Bira's.

She watched him too and saw that, unlike most of the

clan males, who wouldn't tolerate their cubs until they reached a sensible age, Shongshar was delighted with his. He abandoned his usual reserve and played with them as if he were just another cub in the same litter. He let them attack his tail, chew on his ears and climb all over him. Ratha had never heard Shongshar purr, but the continuous rumble that came from his throat as he rubbed his cheek against the little male was the sound of absolute contentment.

Yet, the longer she watched, the more she felt a growing uneasiness about the cubs. They played much as the litterlings in the nursery did: they stalked, pounced and wrestled; but there was something strangely lacking. Their movements were quick and their eyes keen; they seemed to notice everything that moved. But once the object, such as a swaying flower or their father's tail, had been attacked and subdued, it held no further interest unless it moved again.

The litterlings in the nursery also were attracted by things that moved, but after the first clumsy pounce, the cub's expression would change from the excitement of the hunter to the intent curiosity of one who hungered to understand its world. The litterlings' eyes always held questions, even if their tongues were not yet ready to ask them.

Being careful not to disturb the three, Ratha edged closer so she could see more clearly. Shongshar's eyes were glowing with affection and happiness as he tumbled the cubs about with his big paws. Their eyes were alive with momentary excitement, but there was nothing more. Trying to fight the chill creeping over her, Ratha stared hard until her own eyes ached, but she could see nothing. No questions, no hunger . . . no light. As much as she desperately wished to deny it, she knew Bira's instincts had been right.

She felt as though she were looking at cubs who had been stricken with sickness and were soon to die. The sight of them suddenly made her belly churn as it did when she smelled rotten meat; she hated herself for her feeling. Now she knew why Bira couldn't nurse them. If she had forced the young mother to care for these cubs, she would certainly have killed them and then run from the clan in shame and despair.

"Clan leader!" Shongshar had caught sight of her. Ratha gathered her feelings together and put them away. She forced herself to approach him.

"I see that they're thriving on Fessran's milk," she said, unable to think of anything else.

"I'm grateful to her for nursing them." Shongshar stopped and looked troubled. "I don't understand what's wrong with Bira. How could she leave such fine cubs as these? Look how quick and strong they are."

Ratha knew she didn't have to answer him. As clan leader, she didn't have to answer anyone if she didn't want to. She could just mumble something vague and walk away. She looked up into his eyes. The happiness had gone, replaced by the shadow of the same pain she had seen in Bira's. Inwardly she hesitated, knowing that what she must say next would only add to his hurt.

"Shongshar, do you remember the promise you made to me the night you were given your name?"

His ears twitched as if he wanted to lay them back and hiss at her. "Yes," he said harshly. His eyes widened, becoming frightened, almost pleading. "Clan leader, isn't it too soon to tell? I'm sure my cubs will have the light in their eyes when they are older. You can't judge them now. Please, give them some time. I know what Bira thinks, and she's wrong; I know she is."

Ratha wanted to turn away from him, but she forced herself to stay where she was and show no expression. "Do you regret that promise to me?" she asked him.

"No. There was no other choice. If I hadn't come to you, I would have died," he said simply. "But I thought it would be easy to give up my cubs. I never knew how I would feel about them."

Thakur knew, she thought. *That was the reason he was worried.*

"I won't judge them now," she said, looking directly at him. "You are right; it is not yet time. But the time will come when I must judge them and you must accept my decision."

His tail drooped and he looked at the ground. "I understand, clan leader."

He said no more and went back to playing with the cubs, but his movements seemed slower and less spirited. Ratha found it easier not to watch as she went away.

The following day, Ratha visited the nursery. The weather seemed to share her stormy mood. Spring had retreated back into winter, with gusty winds that blew her fur backward and stole the warmth from her coat. Despite the weather, the mothers had brought their cubs out; two females were looking after a large collection of active youngsters.

Most of the cubs had mastered the skill of walking and were now attempting to run. The nursery enclosure was full of spotted bodies hurtling from one side to the other. Ratha watched their antics until she heard someone coming toward her from the opposite direction. It was Fessran, carrying one of Bira's cubs in her mouth. She had a meaningful look in her eyes that said she was not just bringing the cub out to play. Ratha had almost been expecting something like this. Although Fessran had continued to care for Bira's cubs, she missed her own and the strain of worrying about two litters, in addition to her duties as Firekeeper leader, was making her curt and short-tempered.

Behind Fessran, Ratha saw Shongshar with the other. "Drani," Ratha heard Fessran say to one of the two other females who were there, "you have so many litterlings that a few more shouldn't trouble you. I'll make sure Bira takes her turn here since these are hers."

Fessran backed out, allowing Shongshar to slither through the narrow cleft between the rocks and deposit the second cub. Drani hissed at the unexpected entry of a male and Shongshar hastily retreated, tailfirst.

"If you see Bira," said Fessran irritably, "tell her she can feed her own wretched cubs. I want mine back." Then she was gone.

Ratha settled down to watch Bira's youngsters as they made their first attempts to enter the group. Unexpectedly, Shongshar hopped up beside her. Drani looked at him and growled.

"Oh, stop it. He isn't going to hurt them," Ratha snapped.

Shongshar sent Ratha a grateful look as he found a seat on the boulder. The wind teased his silver fur and spread the hairs of his tail against the rock. He leaned down, picked up his little female cub by the scruff and began washing her. When he was finished, he put the litterling back in the nursery.

Another cub pattered up to her and tried to touch noses. She shook herself and walked away. The other youngster followed, trying to sniff her tail. With a silent snarl and laid-back ears, she jumped on him and seized his ear. With a squeal, the other cub backed away dragging her with him.

"No, no, no!" the clan-cub cried shrilly, using the only word he knew. Finally he managed to shake her off and retreated, looking totally bewildered.

"Come here," Shongshar growled at his daughter. She gave him one glance and then bounced away beyond reach of his paw. Drani had to catch her and deliver her back to her father. He took her by the scruff and set her between his paws while Ratha watched. "No," he said sternly. "No. You shouldn't do that to the other cubs."

She looked at him blankly and struggled to get free. When Shongshar put her back in the nursery, she promptly attacked another litterling and paid no attention to his scolding. It took a sharp cuff from Drani to free the victim, and the culprit was again delivered to her father.

"She's not used to other cubs," Shongshar said, with a faintly embarrassed look at Ratha. This time, he kept the cub in front of him, giving Ratha a good chance to study her closely. Her eyes were a gray-blue, with odd orange flecks. She was definitely larger and stronger than the other litterlings, but her stare was as flat and unfocused as that of a newborn whose eyes had just opened.

Ratha suspected that Shongshar couldn't control her because she couldn't understand his words. The only language she knew was that of growls and cuffs. She wasn't surprised when Shongshar took his daughter by the nape and left the nursery. He reappeared a short time later and picked up the young male.

CHAPTER 9

RATHA WAITED before she decided to go after Shongshar. *He must know by now that his cubs will never bear names*, she thought. *Bira knows and she has cut herself off from them. He must do the same or leave clan ground.*

The late afternoon sun had slipped behind a cloud and the rocks beneath her were starting to chill. Wearily she rose and left the nursery, seeking the path to Shongshar's den, a trail her feet were coming to know too well.

He was there, lying across the entrance to the lair as if guarding the way in. Two spotted faces peered out over his back. He lifted his head, showing his profile, and his lip drew back to expose the length of his fangs. He did not look at her.

Ratha sat down, keeping her distance. She waited as the shadows of trees and bushes lengthened, spreading across the ground to the mouth of the den. Her own shadow crept with the others until it touched him.

The wind shifted, blowing his scent to her. She smelled the pungent odor of anger and the bitter acrid scent of despair. She rose and took one pace toward him. The orange glow in his eyes deepened and his nape lifted. Fear struck at her and she fought it aside.

"You have long fangs, Shongshar," she said. "They

could easily find my throat. Killing me would not change the truth about your litterlings."

"It is not you I would kill, clan leader," Shongshar answered in a low growl.

Ratha's gaze hardened. "If you seek revenge on Bira, you are wrong. She is clan born. Had she taken someone other than you—"

"It is not Bira's fault. I know that."

Her fear eased, but she remained wary. "Bira will not return to these cubs. Now that you know what they are, you must abandon them and never think of them again."

The little female started to climb over Shongshar's back. He took her by the scruff, laid her down between his paws and began licking her, even though she smelled as though she had already been washed. Ratha sensed this was his answer.

At last he looked up at her and said, "I didn't know how I would feel about my cubs when I made you the promise that gave me my name. I didn't know how hard it would be." His eyes added the accusation, *You can't know how hard it is, clan leader.*

Her belly ached for him in his sorrow. "You think I ask you to give up your cubs without knowing the bitterness of it?" she asked. He had begun licking the female cub again, but he stopped and laid a paw over her.

"I will tell you something," Ratha said to him. "I have told it to only one other among the Named. I bore a litter of cubs like yours. I took a male who came from outside the clan, like you. When I realized that my young were witless, I nearly went mad." The words poured out of her as the memory came flooding back. "I attacked my mate and tried to kill one of the cubs. He drove me away. Later, he died. I don't know what happened to the cubs; they are probably dead now."

Shongshar lay, looking at her in silence while the shadows crept over his coat. His daughter squeaked and he hushed her. "So you know what this is like." He nudged the cub, who gave Ratha a wide-eyed stare, then blinked and yawned.

Ratha found it difficult to keep her gaze steady. "Yes, I do," she answered finally. "I'm . . . sorry."

He looked away. "What must I do now if I choose to obey you?"

"Take the cubs far away from clan ground and leave them. Or, if you choose not to obey me, you may leave the clan tonight and take them with you." She paused, letting him absorb her words. "I will return to your den tomorrow morning. Either way, if you stay or leave, the cubs must be gone."

"And if I choose to go?"

Ratha swallowed. "Then we will lose the best fire-tender we have ever trained. Your name will be given to the eldest male in the next litter that is born and you will again be the orange-eyed one among the Un-Named."

She got up. The shadows were fading with the coming twilight. "Despite everything, I wish you well, Shong-shar," she said and hoped he couldn't see how she had begun to tremble.

She suddenly wanted to be with someone who could give her comfort, or at least some understanding and companionship. *Thakur*, she thought, *I need you. I know we have disagreed, but don't turn away from me now . . . please don't turn away . . .*

The desire to see the herding teacher became an over-whelming hunger that sent her flying down the dark-ened trail in search of him.

"Watch out, clan leader!" came a familiar voice out of the dusk; she saw a pair of green eyes ahead on the trail. Ratha stopped so fast to avoid a collision that she skidded on wet leaves and fell on her side. Her breath burning in her throat, she hauled herself to her feet.

She forgot her embarrassment and her soggy flank as Thakur's voice and scent reached her. The green eyes blinked. Another, smaller pair glowed momentarily and Ratha made out the shape of the treeling's face between the outline of Thakur's ears.

The herding teacher came forward to touch noses with her. "Where were you going in such a hurry?"

"To find you," Ratha gulped. "You were right about Shongshar. Bira's cubs are witless. You were right and I didn't listen," she cried. "Oh, I wish I had!"

Thakur was quiet for a while and his silence tore at her in a way worse than angry words could. When she thought she couldn't bear it any longer, he said, "Come with me to my den. We'll talk there."

Gratefully she padded after him until they reached his lair. He stood aside to let her in and then followed.

"I knew Bira had abandoned her litter," he said as she curled up with the earthen wall of the den against her back. The rich smell of soil and leaf-mold mixed with his scent made her feel better.

"Their eyes are empty," she said, feeling her voice growing steadier. "I know. I looked at them."

"There is no chance that you are mistaken?"

"How could I be wrong, when my own cubs were like that? I'll never forget my daughter's eyes. I imagine Bira won't forget hers either." Her voice was heavy with self-accusation.

"She'll get over it, in time. You did."

Ratha laid her head on her paws. "I did until seeing Shongshar's cubs brought it all back."

"What have you told Shongshar?"

"I reminded him of his promise to me and gave him the choice of abandoning his cubs in order to stay, or taking them with him and leaving the clan."

"Can he take them?" Thakur asked.

"I think so. They were still nursing, but Fessran was starting to feed them chewed meat. He can't give them milk, but he can chew meat for them."

She heard the soft sound of the herding teacher's tail brushing the ground as he curled it around himself. "When does Shongshar have to make the choice?"

"I said I would come to his den tomorrow. If the cubs are still there, I suppose I will have to take charge of them myself." She sighed unhappily at the thought of that possibility.

She heard an odd shuffling noise and then Thakur saying softly, "Go on, little friend. She knows you. She won't hurt you."

She felt the treeling's paws on her hind foot and held still as Aree hopped up onto her leg and walked up her flank to her back, where he began grooming her fur. Aree's touch was so gentle and careful that she wondered if the treeling knew she was upset.

"The longer I have Aree, the more I think he knows what I'm feeling," said Thakur, and his voice was warm with affection for the treeling. "He doesn't speak, but he seems to say things with his paws."

"He is very gentle. I hope he doesn't mind that I'm

a bit wet." Ratha felt her tenseness seeping away and stretched her mouth wide in a great yawn. "I just had a funny thought."

"What?"

"Aree grooms me the way you would if you had his clever little paws. Maybe he's got some of you in him."

"Perhaps," said Thakur softly. "Do you feel better?"

"A little. I wish he could groom out all my bad feelings along with the ticks and the fleas."

"Not even a treeling can do that."

Ratha drew in her breath and let it out in a huge sigh, lifting the treeling up on her ribs and letting him sink down again.

"Are you thinking about tomorrow?" Thakur asked, after he had been quiet awhile.

"Yes. I hope Shongshar's cubs are gone when I reach the den. I'll still have to face Fessran and tell her what has happened, but I'd much rather do that than have to take them out and abandon them myself."

"I'll come with you, if you want."

"I thought you were angry with me," she said, surprised.

"Not any more." He paused. "If you do have to take the cubs, you can't carry both of them at once."

"Thakur, you don't have to," Ratha answered, ashamed and grateful at the same time. "This is my responsibility."

"The responsibility belongs to all of us," he said as Aree finished cleaning Ratha's fur and climbed down from her back. She felt warmed, comforted and ready to sleep. Perhaps she would be able to face the coming day after all, she thought.

She woke early, unsure of what had roused her. It might have been a bird trilling outside or the faint morning light filtering into the den. She buried her nose in her tail and tried to shut her eyes again, but it was useless. Thoughts of the task that lay ahead stole sleep away. All she could do was watch and wait while the gray light outside grew stronger and Thakur's ribs rose and fell with his slow breathing. Aree, curled up against his belly, looked like a small cub with dusky brown fur.

The treeling began to stir. Thakur twitched and moved in his slumber. She hoped he would wake soon; it was nearly time to depart for Shongshar's den. When he settled down again and began to snore, she reached out a hind foot and poked him. He grumbled a sleepy protest, but his eyes opened and, when she stepped over him on her way out of the den, he quickly came to life.

A ragged fog lay along the ground and patches of mist hung around the few stands of trees. Thakur crawled out of the den with Aree wobbling and yawning on his back. The treeling eyed the weather with distaste and fluffed his fur.

The moist air held scents well and before Ratha reached Shongshar's den she knew he and the cubs would still be there. Someone else would also be with them. Fessran's odor and footprints were fresh, telling Ratha that the Firekeeper leader had taken the same path earlier in the morning.

"I think Shongshar came to get her," Thakur said, from behind Ratha. "His scent is alone on one side of the trail and mingled with hers on the other." Aree contributed a sneeze to the conversation and then shook itself.

Ratha glanced back and wondered whether Thakur should bring his treeling on an errand such as this. She was so grateful for his presence that she decided not to say anything. No one would notice anyway; the creature had become so much a part of him. If Shongshar became angry and forced a fight, Thakur would send his companion up into the nearest tree.

"Even so," she said to him as they approached, "you let me go first."

She saw Shongshar waiting outside the den. His feet and legs were lost in the white swirl of ground fog and the silver in his coat blended into the gray mist. His eyes were the only part of him she could see clearly and they burned at her with a mixture of pain and defiance.

"I couldn't abandon them," he said in a low growl. "I tried, but I just couldn't do it."

Ratha faced him directly. "Do you wish to stay with us?"

"I came to the clan because it was the only way I could survive. There is nothing for me outside."

"You have disobeyed me," Ratha said. "The cubs are still here and so are you. However, if you stand aside and let me take them you may keep your name and your place among us."

He moved away from the mouth of the lair and stared away as she passed him. "I'm sorry, Shongshar," she said but he gave no indication that he had heard.

She bent her head and crawled inside the den. A warm, milky scent met her nose. Enough light entered the lair so that she could see Fessran stretched out with Shongshar's young at her teats.

"They won't be nursing much longer," she said. "I've begun to feed them chewed meat, but they still need a little milk."

"I thought you weren't going to care for them any more."

"I wasn't." Fessran replied. "But when Shongshar came

and asked me again, I couldn't refuse him. Why aren't you doing something about getting Bira to nurse them?"

Ratha braced herself and said in a flat voice, "Bira is not coming back to them, Fessran. Hasn't Shongshar told you what I said to him last night?"

The Firekeeper narrowed her eyes and curled closer about the litterlings. "So you are going to take them to die. I didn't believe you could do such a thing."

Ratha lost her temper. "Oh, stop trying to fool yourself! You've looked at those cubs and you know as well as I do that there is nothing in their eyes." She stopped, trying to calm herself. "Didn't Drani tell you about the trouble in the nursery?"

"Yes," Fessran admitted, looking down at the floor between her paws. She sat up as the restless cubs continued to paw at her belly.

Ratha leaned forward and opened her jaws to take the little male by the scruff. Fessran blocked her, snarling. "No! I have given these cubs my milk. I don't want them to die."

Ratha crouched, her own nape raised, lips pulling back from her teeth.

"I . . . I just think you should give them a little more time, that's all . . . ," Fessran faltered, embarrassed by her sudden flare of anger.

"And you think that it will be easier then? When you have nursed them longer and begun to think of them as yours?" Ratha hissed.

"No. I know they are Bira's."

"But you will still want to see them kept and raised, for Shongshar's sake."

The Firekeeper stared back, her eyes reflecting the light from the lair's entrance.

"Fessran, I would do you no kindness by allowing you to keep them. What will happen when these cubs grow up and you have to face the truth about them? What will happen when the mating season comes? We won't be able to keep them from mating, any more than we could keep Shongshar from it. Do you want to see more litters like this? Do you want to birth cubs like this?"

"No!" Fessran cried. "No, not if you are right about them. But you could be wrong."

Ratha snatched the little male and placed him so that the light from outside the lair fell across his face. "Go on, look at him," she hissed. "Look at him and tell me if you really think I'm wrong." She seized him by the scruff and held him up before Fessran.

The cub hung in her jaws, making no effort to struggle. Fessran peered into his face, studying him intently. Something like pity and revulsion came into her eyes and she turned her head away.

"All right, take him," she said harshly. "Take the female, too; she's the same."

Ratha put the cub down long enough to say, "Go back to your family, Fessran. Go back to your little daughter who is starting to talk. Think how proud you will be when you bring your cubs before the clan to be given names."

She picked the litterling up and carried him from the den.

Outside, she paused in front of Shongshar and put the cub on the ground to free her jaws. "These cubs are yours," she said. "If you still want to take them and abandon them yourself, I will trust you."

"No, clan leader," he answered. "You were the one

who asked for that promise. You have said my cubs must die. I can't fight you, but I won't help you either."

She took a breath. "All right. They are my responsibility now. I accept that."

She picked up the cub again, but Shongshar stood, blocking her way. His orange eyes burned with grief, but what frightened Ratha was the sudden hate that flared in their depths. It was as if she were looking into the eyes of an old bitter enemy. Ratha felt her nape and back itch as the hair lifted; she narrowed her eyes and growled, sweeping her tail from side to side. Shongshar moved out of her way, but as Ratha passed him she sensed that she had not won the confrontation, she had only delayed it.

Fessran crawled out of the den, her coat rumpled. Without looking at the clan leader, she said, "Come with me, Shongshar. I am having trouble being a Firekeeper leader and raising a family at the same time. Cherfan isn't interested in my cubs. If I share my family with you, it will help both of us."

Shongshar lowered his head and paced to Fessran's side. Neither of them looked back at Ratha as they left.

When Shongshar and Fessran had gone, Thakur came out of the brush and fetched the female cub from the lair.

Carrying the cubs in their mouths, the two left clan ground and trotted toward the hazy shapes of the mountains beneath the rising sun. Ratha's jaw was soon aching from straining against the male cub's weight, but she forced herself to go on carrying him, without stopping to rest. Something told her to get these litterlings as far from clan territory as possible.

Part of her started to go numb as she traveled, and it

wasn't just her jaw. Her legs seemed to go on by themselves while her mind functioned only enough to choose the path. The litterlings, seemingly dazed, never cried or struggled, which made them seem more like lifeless burdens than living creatures.

For the rest of the day Ratha and Thakur traveled over plains and foothills until they reached the mountains. Among the pine forests that covered the lower slopes, they found a stream leading up through a shallow canyon until it entered a sheltered meadow. The surrounding canyon walls protected the meadow from wind and the stream lay close by. When the two saw the enclosed pasture, they knew they had come far enough.

As soon as Thakur let the female cub down, she began stalking a large beetle that clung to a swaying stem. She wriggled, pounced, and then Ratha heard her jaws crunch on the insect. The litterling grimaced in disgust at the taste but she gulped it down.

Ratha stared at her, then at Thakur as he said, "Hmm. If she can eat insects, there is a chance that she and her brother may survive here."

"Maybe. Fessran said they had begun to eat chewed meat."

She watched the cubs as they romped around their new home. When they reached the far end of the meadow, she felt Thakur nudge her. "We should go now," he said softly.

He trotted away downstream and, after one last look at Shongshar's cubs, Ratha followed.

She said little on the journey back to clan ground. Although there was some hope that the abandoned young might survive, she knew she couldn't risk telling Shongshar where they had been left. Thakur led the way back and she paced after him, wondering if she would ever lose the weariness of body and spirit that had crept over her, numbing her feelings.

CHAPTER 10

FOR A WHILE AFTER Thakur and Ratha returned to clan ground, he noticed that she was unusually subdued and did not appear among the Named any more often than she had to. She spent much time in her den, her head resting on her paws, her eyes staring ahead at nothing.

"It would have been no easier for me if Shongshar had taken his cubs out and abandoned them," she muttered in response to Thakur's gentle questioning. "It was I who allowed him into the clan to sire those cubs and it was I who decided he must lose them. I wish I could forget that they were ever born, but I keep seeing those little faces before me."

"You didn't kill the cubs," Thakur pointed out. "We chose a place for them where there is food and they will be safe."

"Until the next hungry beast comes along. It doesn't really matter. Shongshar thinks they are dead and so does everyone else who knew about them. Only you and I know that they may survive, at least for a little while."

She sighed, laid her head back on her paws and stared

away again, not noticing when Aree hopped up on her and began to groom her pelt. Thakur called the treeling back again, knowing that Ratha's distress was something she would have to come to terms with by herself; he couldn't help her. He wondered if the faces she saw in her waking dreams were those of Shongshar's cubs or of her own lost young.

Gradually she came out of her lassitude, but whether she had resolved her feelings or just buried them, Thakur couldn't tell. As much as he wanted to stay with her and comfort her, he had other duties that called him. The cubs in the spring litters were now old enough so that he would soon have to begin training some of them as herders.

"It's too early to wake up," Thakur grumbled, opening one eye at his treeling. Aree cocked his head at him and evaded his sleepy paw. For some reason the creature was unusually frisky. On all fours he galloped to the threshold of the den, poked his nose out, galloped back and leaped on Thakur. The creature pawed his fur and told him, with various treeling noises, what he thought of those who snored in their dens while there was such a beautiful morning outside.

The scolding, plus the impact Aree had made when he landed on him, brought Thakur fully awake. "I'm feeding you too much," he growled at the treeling. "You're getting heavy." The treeling had grown rapidly, reaching his adult size. Now when Aree stood beside Thakur on all fours, his back reached the level of the herding teacher's belly. With his legs and tail outstretched, he could extend himself from Thakur's shoulder to withers.

Aree looked at Thakur with such wide soulful eyes that

he knew he must feed his creature. The herding teacher crawled wearily out of his den and found a dead tree that was covered with bark-beetles. Aree climbed up and munched on the insects until he was sated.

Thakur's belly was still comfortably full from the previous day's herdbeast kill, so he would not have to eat for a few days. He shivered as the cold in the early morning air crept into his coat. The mothers would eventually bring their cubs to the meadow and the first day's teaching would begin, but it was still much too early.

He considered returning to his den, but the treeling was still lively. Aree would never let him go back to sleep. He decided instead to take a walk out to the meadow. Some Firekeepers might still be on duty and he could warm himself at the guard-fires.

Only a single fire was still going when he got there, and he could see that the Firekeeper was getting ready to put it out. During winter, the guard-fires burned night and day, but in summer they were only needed in darkness, or when an attack threatened the herds.

He quickened his pace and called to the Firekeeper. He had not expected that it would be Bira.

She greeted him with a nose-touch and asked when he was to start teaching.

"This morning, but not for a while," he answered. "My treeling got me up."

"Could Aree groom my tail?" asked Bira, glancing at the treeling. "I didn't take care of myself for a while and now I've got some wretched burrs that I can't get out with my teeth."

"I think Aree wouldn't mind." Thakur nosed Aree off his back and Bira spread her tail along the ground. She still looked a bit thin and worn, but the fact she had begun to care about how she looked told Thakur that she was recovering from the shock of learning that her young were witless.

"Are the cubs gone?" she asked suddenly.

Thakur hesitated. "Yes. I helped Ratha take them away."

"Don't tell me where. I don't want to know." Her tail twitched beneath Aree's paws. "I'll have another litter next spring. Shongshar will have to go away when the mating season comes again, won't he?"

"I suppose he will," the herding teacher answered. Perhaps Shongshar would accompany him on his annual journey away from the clan. The prospect of having a partner during his yearly exile was something he might welcome to help ease the loneliness of being away. However, he reminded himself, his own retreat was self-imposed. Shongshar's might not be. Ratha certainly didn't want any more empty-eyed litters born on clan ground.

Bira dug her claws into the dirt and grimaced as Aree pulled hard at a tangle in her tail. The treeling wrapped his own tail around hers, to steady himself. He gave a tremendous yank and the burr came free. Aree held the hair-covered thing up in his paws and Bira sighed with relief.

When the treeling had finished grooming Bira, he climbed back on Thakur and cleaned his own coat. She yawned and then began scuffing dirt on the flickering fire.

"Wait," said Thakur. "It's early and I'm still cold. Why don't you let me keep the Red Tongue for a while?"

Bira looked doubtful. "The ashes should be buried. Fessran said that was important."

"I'll bury them when I've warmed myself. Look at Aree. He's shivering too. After all, he did get that burr out of your tail." He nudged the treeling and Aree responded by giving Bira a mournful look.

"All right. Since the other Firekeepers are gone, I'll let you have it. But . . . don't let Fessran know. She's becoming strict with us about the proper care of the fire-creature. She wasn't that hard on us before, but she is now. I think she's been listening to Shongshar a lot lately." Bira wrinkled her nose. "Too much if you ask me."

Mildly surprised at this, Thakur promised and Bira trotted off, swinging her tail and yawning. He curled up near the fire, which had fallen into embers with a few ragged flames licking charred branches. Aree sat on Thakur's flank, gazing at the fire. He noticed that the treeling had stopped fidgeting and grown unusually quiet.

All creatures except the Named feared fire and would not come close to it. Even Aree had huddled in Thakur's fur when he had first brought his new companion near the Red Tongue. Now Thakur wondered if his treeling might have gained some of the same understanding that allowed the Named to tame their fear of the fire. It was ridiculous to suggest that treelings could think as well as the Named did, but Aree had shown surprising cleverness and interest in things other than food and grooming. The treeling also seemed to be aware of Thakur's feelings; something the herding teacher did not expect from a creature he thought of as an animal. Dapplebacks and three-horns were animals too, but they were kept to be eaten. Aree was different.

There was no fear in the treeling's eyes as he gazed at the fire. Even before Aree moved, Thakur sensed that he was about to do something he had never done before. The herding teacher held himself still, but not stiff as Aree climbed down from him. The treeling crouched in the ash-flecked dirt in front of the fire, staring into the flames with a curious intensity. He lowered his muzzle and blinked against the heat. He reached toward the flame with a paw.

Thakur thought at first that Aree was about to make the same mistake that young cubs often did when they encountered the Red Tongue for the first time. They would try to touch the flame itself, not realizing that the most visible part of the fire-creature was the most insubstantial. He readied himself to snatch Aree away if he should try to grasp the dancing flame. But the treeling's paw stopped and descended to a stick that was lying with one end in the coals.

Thakur felt his heart jump and begin to race. Now he understood what he had sensed upon finding the injured creature on the trail: the possibility that those clever little paws might serve the Named in the most difficult task the clan had attempted, the mastery of the Red Tongue. He held in his breath as the paw touched the unburned shaft of the stick and closed around it.

Embers broke open, showing their glowing centers as Aree dragged the stick from the fire. As he lifted the branch to his eyes, the tiny flame on the end sank down and died, leaving only the red and orange coals amid the black scale that had been bark. The treeling brought the end to his face and studied it intently. He reached up with its other paw as if to touch the glowing wood, but the heat warned his fingers away.

Softly, carefully, Thakur began to purr. He didn't know why the treeling had taken the stick from the fire and, at this point, he didn't care. He only wanted Aree to know that this act had pleased him so that the treeling might be encouraged to do it again. Aree's eyes brightened when he heard the purr and he ambled over to Thakur on three legs, still holding the stick. The coals had faded to ash.

"*Aree?*" the treeling said, as if still unsure of whether he had done anything worthy of praise. With licks and nuzzles, Thakur assured his companion that he was very pleased indeed. He made such a fuss over Aree that the treeling tossed his branch aside and rubbed himself against him, curling and uncurling his tail with delight. When some of Aree's exuberance had worn off, Thakur retrieved the stick and offered it to the treeling.

Aree quickly discovered that accepting the stick earned him more licks and nuzzles. For a while, Thakur played a simple game with his companion, passing the charred branch back and forth between them: from teeth to paws and then back again. When Aree began to tire of that, Thakur decided he was ready to try a simple test to see if the treeling would repeat his previous action.

He took the stick and placed it on the fire, in the same position it had originally been in. He moved slowly, letting Aree follow everything he did. When the stick was in place, he picked it up in his jaws, took it out and replaced it carefully. He did this several times as Aree watched. Once he was sure the treeling understood, he put the stick back in the fire again, but instead of grasping it with his teeth, he used his pawpad.

The wood only rolled under his clumsy swipes. With an impatient chirp, the treeling reached underneath Thakur's foreleg, seized the stick and pulled it out. With a gesture almost like a flourish, Aree presented him with the stick as if to say, "This isn't so hard if you have paws like mine. See?"

Thakur licked the treeling until he was damp and

rubbed against him until Aree's coat was thoroughly rumpled. The creature's ability had surpassed his hopes. The treeling had grown large and strong enough to handle all but the heaviest branches. Thakur knew that with enough time and patience, Aree could be trained to handle the Red Tongue with greater safety and skill than the best Firekeeper among the Named.

Thakur felt the sun's warmth on his back and realized the mist had burned off. Soon the mothers would be bringing their cubs to the first training session for young herders. Quickly he nosed Aree onto his back and scuffed dirt on the remains of the Red Tongue. He still had to get the teaching herd ready before the cubs arrived.

He kicked a last spray of dirt on the embers and galloped away. Tomorrow he wouldn't be angry if Aree woke him up early. In fact, he would be the one to wake the treeling. He would probably be able to talk Bira into letting him have the fire again and then he would see what else Aree could do.

Once Aree's training had begun, Thakur was eager to continue. He thought that, after the first surge of enthusiasm, the treeling might become balky and unwilling to brave the morning chill, but that never happened. Perhaps Aree had caught the sense of forbidden adventure that Thakur felt each time he left the den in the half-light before dawn.

Aree learned rapidly and was soon responding correctly to Thakur's directions. He found that the sharp sound he made by clicking his teeth together would command the treeling's attention faster than would spoken words.

Soon Aree could extract a branch from the fire and walk around on three legs, holding the lighted torch. Once or twice the treeling tried to transfer the branch from his hands to his prehensile tail, but Thakur quickly discouraged that. Aree tended to pay less attention to things he held with his tail than what was in his hands. Once he had nearly scorched his back by letting the torch droop.

Thakur took great care to be sure that Aree didn't burn or injure himself during the lessons. He didn't want to wake the fear of the Red Tongue that seemed to lie deep in every creature. The treeling sensed that the fire-creature could hurt if it got too close and Thakur reinforced Aree's caution with further training.

By early summer, the treeling could ignite a pile of tinder with a torch taken from the guard-fire. That morning Thakur was elated and praised the treeling endlessly. He caught grasshoppers for Aree until the treeling was stuffed and nuzzled his paws, whose dexterity seemed amazing in comparison to Thakur's clumsy forefeet.

He remembered what Ratha had said to him while Aree was cleaning her fur. "He grooms me the way you would if you had his clever paws." She had only been half-awake when she spoke those words and hadn't really known what they meant. He hadn't either, but now her words brought a half-seen vision of the possibilities of his partnership with the treeling. He stared at Aree as if he had never seen the creature before. A strange feeling prickled up his back from the root of his tail. He suddenly felt afraid, but it wasn't the kind of fear he knew when facing an enemy, even one unknown. It was a fear closer to the one he got when he looked up into the night sky with its burning stars and felt awe and a strange undefined hunger. It was this hunger, rising from somewhere deep within him, that frightened him.

He gazed down at the treeling, who was crouching

between his forepaws, looking up at him with inquisitive eyes. "Teaching you to care for the Red Tongue is only the beginning," he said softly, and he listened to himself as if someone else was speaking. "There is much more we can do together."

He watched the black paws deftly combing the fur on the treeling's tail and sensed the beginning of a freedom he never knew he had been denied. Ratha was right. The skill of those fingers had started to become his own and it was a gift with far more power than he ever expected.

The sun was hot on his back and the sound of cubs squabbling and chasing each other far down the meadow reminded him that he had students to teach. Quickly he quenched the guttering fire and buried the ashes.

The teaching session with the young cubs began and ended late. It was almost dusk when the mothers came to take their litterlings back to their dens. Thakur stayed to care for his small teaching flock until another herder arrived.

"Could you keep my animals separated from the rest?" Thakur asked Cherfan. "It would save me from having to retrieve them from the main herd tomorrow morning." Absently the big herder agreed, but his attention was on something else. A new fire flickered across the pasture near the sunning rock.

Cherfan stared and wrinkled his forehead. "Looks like the Firekeepers are having a gathering," he said finally "Oh, don't worry about your teaching herd. I'll make sure your animals are grazed apart from the others."

Thakur felt annoyed with the Firekeepers. He often liked to climb onto the sunning rock at dusk to catch the last warmth of the sun and watch the moon rise from behind the trees. Well, he would have to find another place tonight, or go and rest in his den. Despite his irritation he was curious about the gathering and decided to wander over and investigate.

The fire was large and cast its light far into the twilight spreading across the meadow. Smoke poured over the grass and billowed up into the sky. On his back, Aree sneezed and shook his head. Thakur's throat stung as he circled upwind, away from the smoke haze. *The Firekeepers have built a fire far bigger than they need*, he thought crossly.

As he approached, he saw someone pacing back and forth in front of the bonfire, while others sat in a group facing it. Thakur swung back downwind, willing to brave the acrid smoke in order to catch the smells of those assembled in the gathering. He recognized most of the adult Firekeepers, including Fessran, Shongshar and Bira. He also caught the odors of some of the cubs. By now, he knew most of their individual scents. Thakur was not surprised to smell Fessran's cubs, Chika and Nyang, among others, but he was surprised that her son Khushi's scent was among them.

Khushi was to be trained as a herder, he thought. The cub had been among the students he taught earlier in the day, although Shongshar had come and fetched him early, saying that Fessran needed him. Thakur was sure it had not been Khushi's own idea to come to the Firekeeper's gathering. He did not smell happy.

The herding teacher caught another scent, so mixed with smoke that it only hinted at who it belonged to. Was Ratha here? Thakur wasn't sure. The darkness, which had now fallen, and the fire's glare made it hard to recognize anyone by sight. Smoke filled his throat again, making him cough, but the roar of the fire overwhelmed any sound he made. Carefully he made his way to the back of the group and sat close enough to see who was standing in front of the bonfire.

It was Fessran and she had stopped pacing. She faced the group and sat down. Shongshar sat off to the side, with Fessran's three cubs. He was watching her intently as she began to speak.

"My first words are for the young ones who seek training as Firekeepers. You are at this gathering tonight because you are the best. You have been chosen to come here because you are the strongest and the cleverest of the cubs born in the spring season. You are here because we who serve the Red Tongue will not accept anything less."

Aree moved restlessly on Thakur's shoulder. Thakur gave him a nudge to quiet him, and then crept further into the gathering, trying to see the faces of those listening. The Firekeepers sat straight, with bristling whiskers and self-satisfied expressions. Most of the cubs looked awed and excited, their eyes glowing in the firelight. Khushi, sitting between his two siblings, lowered his head and nervously licked a front paw.

"You look at the Red Tongue and it frightens you," Fessran continued. "Why? Because it is stronger than you are and fiercer and wilder? Yes! It is a creature far greater than any of us. It can live forever if it is kept fed and it can grow larger than any animal. The fire-creature takes, as its prey, not only the beasts of the forest, but the forest itself, and, when it is angered, nothing between ground and sky escapes its rage."

Fessran's eyes seemed to have a glint to them that was not her own yellow-amber, but a deeper shade . . . almost orange. Something made Thakur look off to the side at Shongshar. He was leaning forward over the cubs, his gaze intent, his eyes narrowed. His jaw moved as if he were speaking the same words to himself and the fire's glare flashed on his sabers.

Fessran continued, "We may warm ourselves before the Red Tongue and see by its light, but we may do so only as long as we are worthy. And how may we prove our worth? By striving to be as strong and fierce as we can. By thinking not of our paws or our whiskers, but of our duty to the Red Tongue. By refusing to show fear even when it claws at our throats and our bellies. That is what the Red Tongue demands of us."

Fessran paused and surveyed the group. Khushi looked more miserable than ever. "Not all of you will be chosen to train as Firekeepers," she said. "I must know which of you are worthy." Her tail twitched restlessly as she curled it over her feet. "Those cubs who think they are brave enough to carry the Red Tongue, come and stand before me."

Some youngsters strutted forward, their tails high and their whiskers bristling with confidence. Others, like Khushi, crept forward nervously, unwilling to be shamed by their littermates. They arranged themselves in an uneven row in front of Fessran. The harsh light of the bonfire made them squint and blink. She paced before the cubs, studying each one in turn.

"Good," she said finally and looked toward Shongshar. "Bring me a torch," she commanded. He lit a dry branch and brought it to her. The cubs' eyes widened and they sat still, their gaze fixed on the Firekeeper.

Thakur tensed. What was Fessran doing?

The Firekeeper swung around, the torch clenched in her jaws. The flame fluttered and roared as she swept it across in front of the cubs' faces.

Several youngsters squealed in terror and fled with their tails between their legs. Others, like Chika, skittered away, turned and faced the flame with ears laid back. A few cubs flinched and crouched, holding their ground. The fur rose along their backs and bristled on their short tails.

Fessran also looked startled, as if she hadn't expected so many of them to flee. Thakur saw her glance toward Shongshar as if seeking reassurance. Again she passed the torch in front of the remaining youngsters, trying to rout them. All but Nyang backed away, hissing.

It was all Thakur could do not to jump into the midst of the gathering and snatch the brand away from Fessran. He only held back by telling himself that she must have a reason for this, however harsh and cruel it seemed.

She gave the brand back to Shongshar, who replaced it in the fire. "So," she said, looking out over the Firekeepers and the shaken cubs. "You see that being chosen to serve the Red Tongue isn't as easy as you thought. Those of you who stayed within the gathering circle have shown you can fight the fear. Return to your places."

"Firekeeper leader," said one cub in a high quavering voice. "The ones who ran away haven't come back yet. Someone should look for them."

Fessran turned to Bira. "Find the litterlings who fled and take them back to their mothers. None of them are worth training."

Bira left. Thakur felt disbelief hit him and drain through him. He had disciplined cubs himself and treated them harshly, but never had he seen youngsters so deliberately terrified and humiliated. Did it matter to Fessran that her son Khushi had been among those who fled?

He looked again at the cubs who remained in the gathering and saw the fright and rage on their faces turn into fierce determination. Perhaps this was Fessran's way of inspiring them, by making them angry enough to fight back and demonstrate that they were worthy to become Firekeepers. Even so, her tactics seemed cruel and unnecessary.

Then he realized that some of the crowd had noticed his presence and other heads were starting to turn. Hastily he ducked down and backed out from among them. He flattened in the grass in the darkness, suddenly aware of his racing heartbeat. Fessran had begun to speak again, distracting attention from him. Quickly he wriggled away on his belly until he was far enough from them to run. As he paused and his eyes grew accustomed to the night again, he saw a form flee from behind the sunning rock.

The figure was slender and lithe, with a long tail. It was gone before Thakur was sure that he had seen it. "Ratha?" he muttered to himself in the darkness, but he wasn't sure. His first impulse was to follow, but the smoky haze that now filled the air made it impossible to track by scent. He decided it would be best to return to his den to rest and think.

On the way to his lair, he visited Ratha's on the chance she might be there. He found it empty. Feeling uneasy, he sought his own den and the refuge of sleep.

CHAPTER 11

THE NIGHT WINDS had blown away the smoky haze and the morning was clear. Ratha lay atop the sunning rock and watched the dawn. She thought about the previous evening and the Firekeepers' gathering. Her ears swiveled back and the tip of her tail twitched as she remembered what Fessran had done to the cubs.

There was no need to frighten them like that, she thought, *nor to build such a large fire. A smaller one would have kept everyone warm.* Her tailtip twitched again. *But warmth wasn't what Fessran wanted from the Red Tongue last night,* she reminded herself.

Ratha hadn't really meant to hide and watch in secret. She had been late and by the time she arrived, the flames of the gathering fire were leaping into the night sky. The Red Tongue's roar concealed her footsteps and its acrid smoke hid her smell. She could hear Fessran speaking, however, and the Firekeeper's words weren't what she expected to hear. The mood of the group was unusually grim and tense, as if they were readying themselves to fight some enemy instead of welcoming the youngsters who were to be trained as Firekeepers. Even the small cubs had serious expressions on their faces, although a few just looked miserable.

She had stopped her approach, sensing that her presence would disrupt what was happening. For a while, she stood still, listening, torn between her wish to approach openly and her need to know more about this gathering. At last, with a pang of regret for her choice, she circled downwind, through the billowing smoke, and found a place behind the sunning rock where she could watch and listen without being noticed.

The sunning rock. She had been there last night and she was here again. If she leaned over the edge and looked down, she knew she would see her own pugmarks in the dirt where she had crouched beside the base of the stone. If she looked the other way, she would see the freshly turned soil mixed with ash where the Firekeepers had buried the remains of the bonfire. This morning, she had squatted there and watered the place before climbing onto the sunning rock, taking some satisfaction in that small act of possession. She turned her back on the site, preferring to look out over the pasture to where the dapplebacks and three-horns grazed, with the herders tending them.

One thought remained in her mind, however, and it kept irritating her like a bone splinter between her teeth. The harshness of the Firekeepers' test had startled her. Although she knew it was necessary to eliminate timid cubs from those who were to be trained, Ratha found herself disliking Fessran's method. The idea was so uncharacteristic of her friend that she wondered if someone else, such as Shongshar, had suggested it.

"*Ptahh!*" Ratha spat, disgusted with herself. "You know better than that. If anyone has her own ideas about things, Fessran does." Yet, as she thought about the Firekeeper leader, she felt uneasy. Fessran had been a staunch friend and her only ally when she had first taken the Red Tongue before the clan. She had rewarded her by giving her the keeping of this new and awesome creature. It was an honor, but it was also a burden, and Ratha had hesitated before she placed it on her friend.

Often Ratha had watched a fly land on the fresh meat of a kill, knowing that one small insect could lay enough eggs to fill the carcass with maggots and taint the meat. Last night she had admitted to herself that the Red Tongue had its own taint, and she was beginning to think that even the stubborn herder who had been made Firekeeper leader was not immune to it.

As she lay there with her thoughts, she heard a rustle in the grass. She pulled her feet underneath her, crouched and faced out in the direction of the sound. Soon she saw Thakur trotting toward the sunning rock with his treeling on his back. He didn't look up and he kept his steady pace, as if he meant to pass by on his way to the meadow's far side.

As he drew near, he swung away from his path and made a small detour that took him near the buried ashes of the bonfire. Again, Ratha could tell that he meant only to glance at the site and trot on, but suddenly he stopped, sniffed and wrinkled his nose. He paced across the ash-flecked soil until he smelled her mark, where she had watered the buried ashes. He grimaced and looked up at the sunning rock.

She felt uncomfortable at having given in to that earlier impulse. Now she had told Thakur, in a way that no words could, how she felt about the Firekeepers' gathering.

"So you were there and you didn't like it either," he said at last.

Either? Ratha narrowed her eyes at him. She flicked her tail, indicating that he should jump up beside her.

When he was there and settled, she said, "I see I wasn't the only one who hid and watched."

"I didn't think a herder would be welcome in that group, and I was right," Thakur answered. "You, clan leader?"

"I might have been welcomed, but my presence would have made Fessran think again about frightening those cubs the way she did."

She could see that Thakur's next words were chosen carefully. In a quiet voice, he said, "You can forbid another gathering like that."

She stared at him in disbelief. "Forbid it? Just because Fessran built the fire too large and scared some of the cubs? They were too young for such a thing anyway."

"Ratha, I know you well enough to tell how you feel about something. Your words may not tell me, but your mark on those buried ashes does."

"*Arr*," she said, feeling foolish. "I was in a bad mood when I did that."

"And Fessran had nothing to do with your bad mood?"

"All right," Ratha snapped. "She did. But let me tell you this: I may not like how she does things, but what she does works. She told me to make Shongshar a Fire-keeper and she was right. We are no longer losing guard-fires because the Firekeepers are too timid. The herdbeasts are safer than they have ever been. That is what is important to me. Fessran has done well and I am not going to interfere with her, so you can dig a hole and bury that idea."

She thought Thakur would lose patience with her, but he only twitched his ears back and then let them come forward again. His eyes held suppressed excitement, as if he had something to tell her but hadn't found the opportunity until now. "Suppose I were to show you another way to master the Red Tongue, a way that doesn't require that cubs have their whiskers singed in order to prove themselves."

She looked at Thakur as he sat there with the treeling on his back. Aree added his gaze to Thakur's and the combination of the two stares made her feel uncomfortable.

"You haven't found such a way . . . or have you?"

"Just follow me, clan leader," he said and jumped down from the sunning rock.

Ratha didn't catch up with him until he was halfway to the farthest guard-fire. She heard him mutter, "Good. Bira hasn't given up on me yet," and he sprinted ahead, leaving her behind once again.

By the time she arrived, he was speaking with Bira. The young Firekeeper gave a start when she saw Ratha and looked back at Thakur as if asking for reassurance.

"You can go," he said. "Don't worry. It's all right."

Ratha watched the yawning Firekeeper trot away, her tail swinging. She noticed that Bira had left Thakur plenty of wood, although the guard-fire was starting to burn low. The wood was in two piles: a large one, carelessly stacked, and a small one that looked like kindling laid for a new fire.

"She shouldn't leave without kicking dirt on the guard-fire and burying the ashes," Ratha said, with a disapproving glance after Bira.

"She knows her duty. I asked her to leave the fire for me. She does that for me every morning. Fessran doesn't know," he added.

"Hmph," Ratha growled. "You should have asked her."

Thakur ignored her. "All right, Aree," he said to his treeling, "let's show Ratha what you've been learning."

She heard several clicking sounds and had no idea where they had come from until she saw Thakur's jaw move slightly. Aree hopped down from the herding teacher's shoulder and bounded over to the large woodpile. He selected a slender branch that he could hold in one paw and returned to Thakur.

He gave Ratha a grin. She glowered back at him, unimpressed. "All right. He can get wood. That will save the Firekeepers some work."

Thakur clicked his teeth again and gave a soft hiss. Aree held up the branch and curled his ringed tail as if asking a question. The herding teacher snapped his jaws together again and Aree, to Ratha's horror and amazement, scampered directly toward the fire.

Her legs acted as fast as her mind did. She was halfway to the treeling when she was suddenly flattened by someone pouncing on top of her. Only the knowledge that it was Thakur kept her from flipping onto her back and raking his belly, and even so she was tempted.

She tried to get up again, but he held her down. He was looking not at her, but at the treeling. "Go on, Aree. It's all right. She didn't mean to frighten you."

"What are you trying to do? Make Aree jump into the Red Tongue?" she hissed.

"No. Watch," said Thakur's voice in her ear. When she stayed still, he got off her and stood alongside.

Aree approached the fire carefully and laid the stick among the coals. When the branch caught, the treeling pulled it out and held it up with the Red Tongue blossoming at the end. Gripping the branch with both paws, Aree shuffled over to Thakur and placed it between his open jaws. Gently Thakur closed his mouth, being careful of the little fingers near his teeth.

Ratha watched in amazement. It was not so much the act itself that drew her attention but the ease with which Aree performed it. It was evident to her at once that the treeling's paws were much better suited to this task than the clumsy jowls of even the bravest Firekeeper.

Thakur growled deep in his throat and opened his jaws. Aree took the lighted brand and placed it back in the fire. Ratha began to get up.

"Wait. He's not finished yet," said Thakur. Again he clicked his teeth and again Aree scampered away to the woodpile. This time the treeling came bounding back on all fours, his ringed tail wound around another stick. He looked up and cocked his head at Thakur with solemn black eyes on each side of his banded muzzle.

"All right, you can do it that way if you want," said Thakur good-naturedly, as if the treeling understood him. He clicked his teeth and made the same hiss as Ratha had heard before. The treeling went to the fire, took the stick from his tail into its paws, and lit the end as he had done before. He held up the small torch to Thakur. The herding teacher left his place and sat beside the pile of kindling.

The treeling inclined his head at him again. "Come on, Aree. I showed you how to do it," he said, leaning forward to coax his companion. After some hesitation, Aree held the torch firmly and shuffled to the pile of kindling. He seemed a little confused about what to do next and Thakur bent down, nudging the treeling's elbow with his nose.

Aree crouched in front of the kindling and poked the lighted brand between carefully laid sticks. The treeling took care not to disturb the arrangement and soon a second small fire was crackling happily beside the first.

Thakur made a purring sound. Aree's eyes brightened and he dashed over to his teacher to receive a reward of licks and nuzzles. He scrambled up Thakur's back and perched there happily, winding his long ringed tail around Thakur's neck.

Ratha's jaw hung open until the wind began to dry her tongue. At last she recovered her voice. "How did you teach him to do that?" she asked.

"The same way I have always taught the cubs herding. When they do something right, I praise them. When they don't, I correct them, and when they are confused, I show them what to do by doing it myself. Aree was already curious about the Red Tongue and I encouraged him."

"And you were careful to make sure he didn't hurt himself. Even so, I didn't know treelings could be so clever. You know that most of the Firekeepers can't light a pile of kindling without knocking it flat. The Red Tongue dies and then they have to set the wood up all over again."

Thakur began kicking dirt on the guard-fire and Ratha helped him bury the ashes. The second fire they knocked apart with their paws and scattered the smoking tinder.

"Well, clan leader?" he asked when they were done.

"Yes!" Ratha said eagerly. "Keep training him. I'll tell Fessran to make you a nest for the fire-creature near your den."

She thought that would please him, but instead a shadow passed across his face, darkening his green eyes. "I'd rather use Bira's guard-fire," he said.

"You don't want to show Fessran what Aree can do?"

"No. Not yet," Thakur said and quickly added, "Aree needs more teaching. You saw how I had to help him. He should be able to do it all himself."

She suspected that he had another reason for wishing to delay, but she decided not to press him. Soon he left to teach his herding pupils and she went back to the sunning rock, feeling more at ease than she had all morning.

Ratha didn't see Thakur again for several days, letting him have time to work with the treeling. She knew that the Firekeepers were planning another gathering and Fessran might repeat what she had done at the previous one.

She made sure she was atop the sunning rock early the next day when Thakur came trotting by with Aree on his back. This time she jumped down and went to him.

"Herding teacher, the Firekeepers are having another gathering soon. I want Fessran to see your treeling before she speaks to the cubs."

She could sense his reluctance, but he finally answered, "Yes, you're right. We should try it. Perhaps I'm wrong about her."

Ratha wanted to ask more questions, but Thakur looked slightly impatient and Aree began to scratch himself.

"Meet me here tomorrow, after your herding pupils are gone," she called after him. "I'll bring Fessran and we'll have the fire ready."

He waved his tail in answer, but the look on his face told her he didn't think they would have much success.

Arrr, he's just being cautious as he often is, she told herself. *I think Fessran will be pleased with Aree.*

The Firekeeper leader arrived in the late afternoon. She brought some others with her, including Shongshar and her eldest son Nyang. Fessran was eager to learn what Ratha had to show them, but even her insistent questions couldn't pry Ratha's secret loose. After the Firekeepers had built the Red Tongue's nest and set the tinder alight, she told them to sit and wait until Thakur came.

At last he padded into the long shadow of the sunning rock, tired, dusty and smelling strongly of herdbeasts. Some of the Firekeepers eyed the treeling and drew back their whiskers. It was not a promising start.

Despite the bad beginning, Ratha grew more hopeful as the demonstration progressed. She could see that the additional days of training had been well used. Aree performed better than he had when she'd seen him the first time. She could tell that the Firekeepers were impressed, but she also sensed hostility, as if they resented the treeling's skill.

Shongshar sat next to Fessran, muttering things in her ear. Each time he spoke to her, the interested expression that had been on her face when Thakur began to show Aree's skills faded a little more, until her expression was as wooden as the others'.

Ratha knew Thakur had anticipated this. He gave her a meaningful glance as he set Aree to laying out kindling for another fire. This task was not something she had seen before and she watched in fascination as the little paws placed each stick carefully against the others, making a perfect nest for the Red Tongue. Not once did the treeling drop a stick or knock the pile over. With Thakur's careful guidance, Aree took a torch from the original fire and lit the new pile.

The Firekeepers' eyes widened despite themselves. Even Shongshar looked impressed, although Ratha was sure he didn't want to be.

Perhaps Aree also felt the challenge from the Firekeepers, for the next thing the treeling did was unexpected. Seizing a stick small enough to carry in one paw, Aree plunged one end in the fire, drew it out and galloped around the Firekeepers on three legs, carrying the Red Tongue. Thakur's whiskers drooped in dismay and he chased after the treeling. That was exactly what Aree wanted. He scampered toward Thakur, leaped up on his back and rode him with the firebrand lifted high in both paws.

As soon as Thakur stopped, Aree bounced down from his back, tossed the firebrand back into the flames and swaggered back, his tail curled high, expecting the usual reward of licks and nuzzles. Ratha could see that Thakur had no choice but to praise the creature. The treeling's antics were not what he had planned, but they were equally astonishing. The Firekeepers' jaws hung open in amazement.

Shongshar, not Fessran, was the first to speak. "Your treeling is skilled, herding teacher," he said, studying Aree closely. The treeling fluffed his fur at him and wound his tail tighter around Thakur's neck. "Did you spend much time teaching him?" Shongshar asked.

"Yes, I did. Aree is clever and learns fast, but he took a lot of work."

"Why did you choose to teach a treeling instead of teaching clubs?"

Ratha saw Thakur hesitate. "I teach cubs herding. I am not a Firekeeper," he said. "I taught Aree because he has a special ability that the cubs do not have. His paws are different from ours: they are made to grasp the limbs of trees as he climbs. He is not as clumsy as the cubs. He doesn't knock things over."

"The cubs understand what they do when they serve

the Red Tongue," said Shongshar softly. "Does your tree-ling?"

"No," Thakur admitted. "He understands only the actions necessary to care for it."

"He does not share the feelings that we have for the fire-creature. He does not know its strength and its power."

"No," the herding teacher replied, his green eyes glowing angrily. "How can you expect a treeling to understand such things? There is no need for him to understand. He just does what you tell him."

"Then he is an animal, like the dapplebacks and three-horns," said Shongshar with a hiss in his voice and a gold glitter in his eyes. "He is witless, like my cubs that you and Ratha took from clan ground. Is an animal to serve the Red Tongue?"

Ratha felt her own eyes narrow and her nape rise. "Enough, Shongshar! It is Fessran I would hear, not you."

The Firekeeper leader lifted her chin and eyed Ratha coolly. "Clan leader, I share many of Shongshar's feelings. You know better than I how fiercely we fought for the Red Tongue in the days when Meoran ruled the Named."

"Yes, you ran with me then and your feelings were your own," growled Ratha. She regretted her words as they left her tongue, for Fessran flinched visibly and her amber eyes took on some of the same hard glitter as Shongshar's.

"The treeling's skill is impressive," she said. "However, I do have some questions. You have only one tree-ling and there are many Firekeepers. Do you intend to catch more treelings and train them in the same way?"

Thakur looked at Ratha. "I hadn't thought about that. I got Aree by accident. He was injured when I found him. It may be difficult to catch others."

"If we accepted Aree and let him do the difficult tasks for us, we would no longer try to do them for ourselves," Fessran pointed out. "What would happen then if the treeling were to run away or get killed?"

Thakur had come to sit beside Ratha and she felt him tense at Fessran's words. "I don't think Aree is going to run away and I am certainly not going to let anyone kill him." He glared back at the Firekeepers.

Ratha decided it was time to interrupt. "There will be no talk of killing," she snapped. "Thakur has offered to share his treeling's ability and you should be grateful."

"Clan leader, we did not mean to offend either you or Thakur," said Fessran. "We think that the treeling's skill is valuable, but there are some problems. After all, Thakur did not know what the creature would do when he snatched up a torch and began running around us. I think you would agree that more training is needed before the treeling can really be trusted."

Ratha tried to control her temper. Fessran might be irritating, but she had made some points. Aree's last display showed that the treeling was still unpredictable, and there remained the problem that there was only one of the creatures. Nonetheless, Ratha was pleased with Thakur for trying to jolt the Firekeepers out of their complacency.

"All right," she said at last. "Thakur, you are to continue teaching Aree. To make things easier for you, Fessran will assign a Firekeeper to build and tend a fire near your den. Do you both agree?"

Fessran glanced at Shongshar and looked uncomfortable. "Is there anyone you would like?" she asked Thakur.

"If you could spare Bira, I wouldn't mind working with her," Thakur answered.

He stayed beside Ratha as the Firekeepers put out their

fire and left. He smoothed his ruffled fur with short angry strokes of his tongue.

"Fessran will let you have Bira," Ratha said as the dusk closed around them.

"She may. I wonder what else she'll do."

Ratha looked at him sharply, but he was only an outline and two eyes in the growing darkness. "She will do as I tell her as long as I am clan leader."

He sighed. "I wish you hadn't put it that way," he said softly and padded away with his treeling on his back.

During the next few mornings Ratha visited Thakur at his den to be sure Fessran was doing what had been promised. Each time she went, she found Bira there along with a well-made little fire and a stack of wood that was always kept full. The young Firekeeper seemed to enjoy watching Thakur teach Aree. Ratha watched her carefully for signs of the same hostility that other Firekeepers had shown, but there were none.

Aree's instruction was progressing well. The treeling seemed to understand that capricious actions, such as those he had performed in front of the Firekeepers, were not acceptable and would result in a scolding. Thakur reported that Aree had become more obedient, and she could see for herself that the herding teacher had managed to accomplish this without breaking the creature's spirit. Every once in a while Aree looked at Thakur with a mischievous glint in his eyes, but the treeling took his task seriously and never deliberately disobeyed.

Ratha watched and felt encouraged. Soon Thakur would be able to show Aree to the Firekeepers again, and they would be unable to find any fault with the treeling's performance. Perhaps she and Thakur could also devise a way to capture more treelings. Aree might be able to lure another one down from the branches. If the captured treeling was a female, she might bear young. Or Thakur might climb one of the fruit trees with Aree and look for a treeling nest that might shelter young ones. If they could find and train more of the creatures, Fessran might be willing to accept the idea.

She made her plans carefully as she rested in her den or lay atop the sunning rock. Each morning she asked Thakur whether Aree was ready. The last time, instead of saying no, he had told her to assemble the entire clan on the following day. This was something for everyone to see, he said. Not just Firekeepers.

On the evening before the assembly was to take place, Ratha visited him to be sure he was prepared. She came just before sunset and was only halfway to his den when she heard someone running toward her on the path. Thakur galloped up to her, his whiskers trembling and his fur on end.

"Aree's gone, Ratha!" he gasped.

Disbelief shot through her. "What? He can't be. You never leave him alone."

"I did. Just for a little while. I left him curled up in my den. I had to get some wood; Bira let the woodpile get low. Thornwood is best, but I can't get into a thicket with Aree on my back, so I left him."

"How long ago?" She began to pace beside him.

"I had just come back from teaching my herding pupils. I left Aree in my den, went to get wood, and when I came back I couldn't find him. I looked everywhere," he added mournfully.

"Did you try to track him?"

"Yes, but there was such a smoky smell in the air that I couldn't follow his scent."

They reached his den. Ratha trotted over to the ashy bed where the teaching fire usually burned. She lifted her nose and sniffed. Thakur certainly was right: the air was too acrid to detect the treeling's scent. Carefully she pawed the dirt and cinders. If the fire had been burning recently, they would still be hot. They weren't.

Then why did the whole place smell like someone had been throwing ashes around, she wondered.

"Where's Bira?" she asked, suddenly.

"She's not here. She only helps me in the mornings. I thought I'd build a fire myself and then get a Firekeeper to light it."

Ratha glanced up at the few trees that stood about the den. Their branches were outlined against the red and gray sunset, but she saw nothing on them that looked like the hunched form of a treeling. She helped Thakur look through the bushes, but neither one of them found anything.

The wind had begun to stir, blowing away the acrid smell in the air, but Aree's scent had faded too. The treeling was gone and there was nothing either one of them could do about it.

Thakur crawled into his den and laid his head on his paws. "It's my fault," he moaned. "I shouldn't have left him alone. Aree, wherever you are, please come back. I miss you."

"Thakur," Ratha said softly, "I have to go and tell everyone that the gathering won't happen tomorrow."

"Tell the mothers they can keep their cubs for the day," Thakur growled. "I don't feel like teaching. I may be doing some other things, such as asking a lot of questions. Maybe I should start now." He raised himself up and started to crawl out of the den, but Ratha put a paw on his back.

"No," she said. "You stay here. If there are any questions to ask, I will ask them and I will bring you the answers."

"I suppose you can get better ones than I can." Thakur laid his head on his paws again.

His dejection and the misery in his voice made Ratha hot with indignant anger. Whoever had taken the treeling or driven it away had done more than deprive Thakur of a companion. They had stolen his hope and wounded him badly.

She licked him gently on the forehead, trying to comfort him in his grief and anger. At last he fell into a troubled sleep and she left, resolving that she would either find Aree or have her revenge on whoever had stolen the treeling.

CHAPTER 12

THE FACE of the sunning rock was lit with orange as Ratha emerged into the night meadow. Against it, she could see the forms of the assembled Firekeepers, and in front of it, someone paced back and forth. Ratha could hear the drone of a voice mixed in with the hiss and roar of the bonfire.

Irritation stung her and quickly turned to anger. The Firekeepers were meeting again without her permission and without her knowledge. Again they had built the nest for their overfed fire right at the base of her sunning rock.

Too angry to feel unwelcome, Ratha galloped across the meadow and pushed her way through the gathered torchbearers until she faced the firelit form in front. She felt the warning touch of fear when she realized that it was Shongshar, not Fessran.

She looked for the Firekeeper leader and found her sitting off to the side. Her eyes were narrowed and cold, but suddenly they opened and a false welcoming expression forced itself onto Fessran's face. That look on the face of one who had been a friend made Ratha's belly twist and she looked away.

She turned instead toward the others and saw Bira sitting behind Khushi, crouching as if she wanted to hide. Nyang was in front of the crowd, gazing at Shongshar with a rapt expression and adoration glowing in his eyes. Someone else also sat in front, someone she had not expected to see.

The herder Shoman turned and stared at her, his eyes filled with uncertainty. Slowly he lowered his head and began to lick his foreleg. The motion drew Ratha's gaze to his leg. She saw an ugly red streak that oozed and glistened in the orange light.

"Clan leader." Fessran rose to break the tension that Ratha's arrival had brought. "I am glad you have come. I was going to send Nyang to fetch you."

Ratha ignored her. "Why is Shoman here? What happened to his leg?"

"Ask him," said Shongshar and looked toward Shoman.

The herder answered, "I . . . was warming myself by the herders' fire. There were no Firekeepers there. I tried to give the Red Tongue more wood, but it grew angry and hurt me."

"You have done wrong, Shoman," said Fessran severely. "Only the Firekeepers may tend the Red Tongue. You should have gone and fetched one of us."

"Why is he here?" Ratha demanded. "If he has done wrong, let Cherfan punish him since he is a herder, not a Firekeeper."

"He has come to make amends," answered Fessran. "He agreed to come and show the cubs what can happen if the fire-creature is angered by carelessness."

Ratha looked again at Shoman. He crouched, huddled, nursing his leg and grimacing in pain. His glance was furtive and resentful. Fear flitted across his face as he caught Shongshar's gaze; she knew he hadn't come here by choice.

"All right!" she cried, suddenly sickened. "The cubs have seen enough. Shoman, go to Thakur and have your wound tended."

Shoman slunk off into the darkness, limping. The look he gave Ratha was still heavy with resentment, but there was a strange tinge of relief in his eyes.

"We are glad you have come, clan leader," said Fessran. "You have seen with your own eyes the danger the Red Tongue presents to herders, who are not trained to care for it properly."

Ratha waited, trying not to twitch her tail. Fessran eyed her and continued, "As leader of the Firekeepers, I am asking you to forbid anyone to approach the Red Tongue unless one of us gives permission. This would prevent any of the herders from injuring themselves as Shoman did."

"I am glad you are concerned about those who provide meat for the clan," she answered, letting a little sarcasm creep into her voice. "However, I don't think the herders would like it if they had to ask a Firekeeper for permission to warm themselves or see by the Red Tongue's light."

"Cubs do not like being forbidden to do dangerous things, but we must restrict them to keep them safe. Those who do not understand the fire-creature's ways should not meddle with it," said Fessran.

Ratha gathered her temper as she faced the Firekeeper leader. "Fessran, I understand your worry and I agree that there is some danger, but I wish to hear from the herders themselves before I make any decisions."

"That is reasonable, clan leader," Fessran answered.

Those who do not understand the fire-creature's ways should not meddle with it. Ratha turned to the group, repeating Fessran's words silently in her mind. Did that include Thakur and his treeling as well as ignorant herders?

She surveyed the gathering, looking briefly into each face, as if she could find an answer there. Some of the Firekeepers answered her gaze directly, some held hidden defiance and others were uncertain or afraid.

"All of you know the herding teacher Thakur and the treeling he carries on his back," said Ratha. "Some of you were at the gathering where he showed us how Aree could tend the fire-creature." She looked meaningfully at each one of them. "I have just spoken with Thakur. The treeling is gone. We can find no trace of him. I came here to ask if anyone has seen him or knows where he might be."

"When did this happen?" Fessran said, and Ratha heard honest concern in her voice.

"This evening. He had to leave Aree in his den while he went to get thornwood. He says he wasn't gone long and when he came back, Aree had vanished. Does anyone know where the treeling is?"

The Firekeepers looked at each other and muttered negatives. Ratha waited.

"Perhaps the tree-creature ran away and returned to his own kind," said Shongshar, after a long silence.

"That is possible, but Thakur and I don't think so."

Fessran crossed in front of the fire and sat down beside Shongshar. "Poor Thakur. He really liked that queer little animal. I didn't think that he should have taught the creature how to play with the Red Tongue, but I didn't want Thakur to lose him." She thought for a moment. "I suppose you are wondering why he disappeared this evening, since we were to see him perform again tomorrow."

Fessran's gaze softened and Ratha felt less irritated with her, although she could not allow her suspicion to relax. Either Fessran knew nothing about Aree's disappearance or she was good at deceit.

"Yes, I was wondering about that," Ratha admitted.

"I tell you honestly that I knew nothing about it until you came to this gathering. I don't think Shongshar knew either." She turned to her companion. "You were with me all day, so there was no way you could have known until Ratha told us."

"I did not know, clan leader," Shongshar said, but Ratha found it difficult to tell whether truth was hiding behind his orange gaze. Fessran had begun to pace back and forth, her tail shaking with indignant anger.

Ratha wondered if she was outraged because Thakur's

treeling had been taken or because her Firekeepers were under suspicion.

"Hear me, torchbearers!" Fessran cried. "What has been done to Thakur is a shameful thing. I have disagreed with him, but he is my friend. If any of you have had a part in this or have knowledge that you are concealing, come forward now."

She strode up and down in front of them, glowering at them. No one moved, except Bira, who shivered.

"Then you are all innocent," said Fessran in a low voice. "If I am wrong and someone is hiding his guilt, then may the Red Tongue burn in his throat until his tongue falls from his mouth in cinders!"

Ratha felt her breath catch in her own throat. For a moment the Firekeeper leader looked like the old Fessran, the friend who had fought beside her against the old clan leader and whose fierce love and loyalty had sustained her during the chaotic days after Meoran's death.

I have no right to judge you, Fessran, she thought suddenly. *We have both changed more than we wished.*

Fessran came to Ratha and looked her directly in the face. "Neither I nor any of the Firekeepers have done such a shameful thing," she said. "You must accept that as truth, clan leader."

"If I can," Ratha answered softly as she turned to go.

Sadly she returned to Thakur and told him that she had learned nothing. Even her suspicions were difficult to justify; for now she felt she had best keep them to herself. It was possible that the treeling had run off to find a mate among his own kind, she suggested.

The next day, she helped him search for the treeling again, but they only saw wild ones who scrambled up to the tops of their trees and clung there in the swaying branches. There was a cull in the meadow that day and Ratha ate as if her belly would never be filled, but she saw that Thakur had no appetite and quickly gave up his place to the one behind him.

He went back to teaching the cubs, but his step was heavy and his scolding harsher than it had been. He closed himself off to all, even Ratha, and he rarely spoke or looked anyone in the face. He seemed to have lost his spirit along with the treeling and he faded day by day until he became like a shadow among the shadows of trees and bushes that fell across clan ground.

Ratha spent much of her time with the Firekeepers. Her major reason for doing so was to prevent gatherings of the sort that frightened cubs, but she also felt she had failed to give the Firekeepers proper guidance in their attitude toward the fire-creature. She did admit to herself that she was a little uncertain about what that attitude should be.

Fessran seemed to welcome this new attention, although Shongshar clearly did not like it. The Firekeeper leader often invited Ratha to come with her at night when she patrolled the ring of guard-fires around the meadow. They frequently had time to talk, and Ratha realized that her position as clan leader had distanced her from the one who had been her most loyal friend.

Summer had come and the warmth of the day stayed into late evening. Only in the hours before dawn did the night grow cold and dew settle on the grass. This was the time when the Firekeepers were weary, when the fires could sink low and the threat of attack was the greatest. Fessran chose this time to patrol, walking from one outpost to the next, seeing that each fire was properly tended and that there was enough wood. She offered encouragement and good spirits to those who stood the early morning guard. Ratha was heartened to see the weary Firekeepers grin at Fessran's teasing. She noticed that her own presence also seemed to cheer some of them.

She was following Fessran across the moonlit grass and had stopped to shake the dew from her feet when a scream tore through the night's silence. She knew in an instant that the cry had not come from any of the herd animals nor from raiders lurking nearby. It was a scream of pain and terror and it had come from the center of the meadow.

Ahead of her, she saw Fessran start and freeze as the cry began again. Then both of them were racing across the grass.

"The herders' fire," panted Fessran as Ratha caught up with her. "Over there by the old oak."

The herders had begun to cluster about the fire that they used to warm themselves. In their midst lay an orange-lit form that jerked and writhed. The head stretched back, the mouth snarled open, and Ratha heard another terrible cry.

She sped past Fessran and skidded to a stop in the middle of the herders. Her belly gave a painful twist when she saw that the distorted face was Bundi's. Cherfan pawed the shuddering young herder, looking frightened and lost.

"Turn him over," Ratha ordered. "Quickly."

As carefully as she could, she helped Cherfan roll Bundi over. As the side of his face and neck came into view, Ratha felt her lips draw back from her teeth. From his cheek to his neck and shoulder, his flesh was blistered and glistening, with ash clinging to charred fur. Even as she watched, the skin of his face began to pucker, drawing the corner of his mouth back.

His eye was swollen shut and both his nose and eyebrow whiskers on that side were gone.

"Take him to the stream," said Fessran, pushing her way through the crowd of herders. "Water can ease the Red Tongue's hurt. Hurry!"

Half-dragging and half-carrying Bundi, Ratha and Cherfan lugged him to the little creek near the trailhead.

"Lay him here, where there is no mud on the bottom," Fessran directed, wading in. "Easy. Hold his nose out of the water."

Ratha bent her head down, trying to see Bundi's face. She felt his breath on her whiskers as he panted rapidly and arched his back in a convulsive shudder. He opened his mouth for another scream, but could only gurgle and cough as water filled his throat.

Ratha caught his nape on the uninjured side and lifted him enough for the water to drain out. Cherfan helped her move him so that he was lying in the shallows with his muzzle on the bank. After a while his breathing became steadier and he managed to whisper that the pain was less.

"Can you take care of him?" she asked Cherfan and Fessran. "I want to go back and look at the fire."

"Poor clumsy cub," she heard Cherfan moan as she climbed out of the stream and shook herself hard. "You shouldn't have gone near the Red Tongue when there was no one there to protect you."

Ratha laid back her ears as she trotted toward the fire. Bundi was awkward, but he wasn't that clumsy, was he? She circled the firebed, examining the ground carefully. It was no use; the herder's tracks and her own obliterated Bundi's and those of anyone else who might have been there. Likewise, the scents of everyone who had been there were too thick for her to detect any suspicious smells.

She could see that the fire had definitely been disturbed. It was lopsided and there was a large imprint in the ash and crushed coals where a body had fallen. Now the question remained: had Bundi tripped over his own paws, or had someone pushed him?

Again, she circled, looking for tracks where the dirt met the grass. She found half of one pugmark and decided that it had been there before the herders had all crowded around Bundi. The print was too large to be Bundi's. It would only belong to one of two males in the clan: Cherfan or Shongshar.

Cherfan had been there when she arrived, she reminded herself. *But Bundi is his own son! I know Cherfan and he could never do such a thing to a cub he sired.* That left only Shongshar.

But even if the print was his mark, when had he left it? He could have been one of those who helped build the herders' fire earlier that evening. Or he could have pushed Bundi. But he seemed even fonder of Bundi than Cherfan was. Neither possibility made much sense.

Was the Red Tongue itself the malignant force? Could Fessran have been right when she suggested the fire-creature could lash out against those who displeased it? Could it have sensed the presence of an ignorant herder, lured him close and then pulled him in?

For a moment Ratha stared at the fire, which was burning steadily as if nothing had happened. *This is a creature we do not understand*, she said to herself, and the thought sent her tail creeping between her legs. Fear crawled through her fur and she suddenly wanted to flee from this alien thing before it reached out and took her in its fierce embrace.

She made her legs stop shaking and swallowed the lump in her throat. There were questions she had to ask and the answers to those would tell her whether to believe that the fire had needed any help to burn poor Bundi.

When she returned to the stream, Fessran was coaxing Bundi out of the water; she even got him to shake himself off a little. He crouched on the bank with Cherfan close against him on one side and Fessran on the other, trying to warm him. Fessran spoke softly, trying to cheer and reassure him. She was so honest in her concern and her eagerness to help that Ratha knew, whatever had happened, Fessran had taken no part in it. Now and then, Bundi burst into shivers, but he seemed to be in less pain. The three of them looked like an odd moonlit lump on the streambank.

Ratha shivered herself as the night wind touched the dampness in her fur. "Can you walk, Bundi?" she asked him. "You should be sheltered in a den. Fessran, will you take him to your lair?"

"Yes, I will, but there is something I want to do first."

"What?"

"Post some Firekeepers at the herders' fire."

Ratha felt surprise and then a touch of annoyance, but she was too drained and a little too frightened to argue. If the Red Tongue was malevolent, she had a duty to guard her people from it.

"All right," she agreed at last.

She knew Fessran sensed her reluctance, for the Firekeeper said, "I'll give Bira that duty. She gets along well with most of the herders. She can choose whom she wants to work with her."

This cheered Ratha. Bira wasn't likely to think herself above the herders or make arbitrary decisions about who could come near the fire and who couldn't.

The young Firekeeper was summoned and soon took up her new post. Several herders eyed her suspiciously, for they were not accustomed to having a Firekeeper in constant attendance. But when the news of Bundi's injury spread, they changed their minds and welcomed her protection.

Fessran took Bundi to her den and made him comfortable there. Ratha looked in on them just before weariness sent her to her own lair. She crawled into it just as dawn was beginning to color the sky, and she quickly fell into a deep and exhausted sleep.

She was not often troubled by dreams, but the events of the night seemed to replay themselves in her mind in a way strangely altered from what she had seen. In her dream, she stood again before the Red Tongue and, as she watched, the fire-creature changed. The flames that licked up toward the sky seemed to bend down and separate, as if they were becoming legs, and their tips became rounded and solid as if they were turning into paws. The heart of the fire elongated into a body. Part of it drew into a ball and made a head with flame-licked ears and red coals for eyes.

She watched in terror as the rear legs formed and a plume of fire swept itself out into a long tail. The creature opened its mouth, showing teeth that had the impossible sharpness of a reaching flame. In its fur were streaks of blue, violet and yellow against a background of searing orange.

Slowly it began to move, and its flame-substance rippled as if it had muscles. It fixed its glowing eyes on her and she shook until her teeth chattered as she felt its endless devouring hunger. Her mind begged her legs to run, but she stayed, paralyzed by fright and a kind of horrified fascination.

The fire-creature lowered its head and placed one foot before the other. It was leaving the den of coals where it had grown and was coming toward her. Now it spoke and its voice had the soft hiss of the burning flame. "Bare your throat to me, clan leader," it said. "Bare your throat to me, for I am the one who rules."

She crouched, drawn and repelled by its terrible beauty. As if in worship, she lifted her chin, showing her throat. The creature that had sprung from the fire's heart approached her and opened its mouth for the killing bite. She felt its breath on her and its whiskers, made of slender tongues of fire, touched her and left searing streaks on her skin beneath the fur. She felt the points of its fangs draw across her throat.

"No!" she screamed and lashed out with all her strength against it.

She awoke with her claws fastened in the wall of her den and her teeth bared. With a grateful sigh of deliverance, she sank down and lay limp until she was sure the horror of the dream had really passed. Her coat was rough and filled with dirt and she could see where she had writhed on the floor of her lair.

Unsteadily she got up and left the den, shaking the earth out of her fur and smoothing her pelt with her tongue. The early afternoon sun shone down through the scattered trees, comforting her with its warmth and golden light.

But she couldn't forget those coal-red eyes that glowed with a hunger that would never be sated. She knew the creature was a dream, but she also knew that dreams often spoke truth. Although she had set herself to master the Red Tongue, she understood that a part of her mind would always look upon the fire-creature with a terror that could not be answered with reason.

When Fessran came to her that evening and asked that Bira be assigned to guard the herders' fire again, it was easy for Ratha to agree. Soon the Firekeeper had that duty regularly. At Fessran's urging, she forbade any of the herders to go near an unguarded flame.

Bundi recovered slowly. His wounds were less serious than Ratha had thought and she credited Fessran's idea of bathing him in the stream. The swelling on his face diminished; the eye that had been forced shut opened again. He could walk, but he limped because the burn extended from his face down his neck to his shoulder and it hurt him to stretch the blistered skin.

He was soon back with the herders, doing what he could and trying to do more. Soon he had recovered full use of his shoulder, but he and everyone around him knew that he would always be disfigured.

Ratha continued to seek an answer to the mystery of Bundi's accident. She questioned him carefully, but shock had driven the memory from his mind and he couldn't recall exactly what had happened. He knew only that he had flung himself out of the firebed and rolled on the ground until someone came.

Shongshar remained politely evasive and Ratha did not want to alienate Fessran by pressing him harder. She was sure Fessran herself had nothing to do with it and if she suspected Shongshar at all, she would have spoken.

CHAPTER 13

FERNS STROKED Ratha's side as she padded through them and along the mossy bed beside the streambank. She startled a frog and heard it plunk into the clear water. Above her, scattered trees spread their branches toward each other across the creek. When the breeze died, she could hear the soft splash of a waterfall that lay farther up the trail.

She was following the little creek up from the meadow to its source in the hills, something she often did when she wandered alone with no destination and a wish for only her own company. She thought wistfully that she would like to have taken Thakur along, but he was busy teaching this morning. His unhappiness over the loss of his treeling would have made him a poor companion anyhow. There was not much she could do to cheer him up; she had already tried. Eventually he would forget his grief, but it would take time.

She felt a little angry with him for retreating into sorrow when she was most in need of his help and support. There was no one she could talk to now. She thought briefly of unburdening herself to Fessran, but their friendship had grown too uncertain. The Firekeeper leader had found a new loyalty, one that was pulling her away from her old ties.

Since the accident, the herders had shunned Bundi, for they viewed his scars as a mark of the Red Tongue's displeasure. The cub, whose awkwardness had made him shy, was becoming bitter and lonely, and the look in his eyes was that of someone much older. The only herder who would work with him now was Shoman, whose leg also bore marks of the Red Tongue's wrath and who suffered the same hostility as Bundi. There was little Ratha could do about the herders' rejection of the injured pair except to demand that it not be shown in her presence.

The trail began to slope upward and Ratha followed it, listening to the sound of the waterfall as it echoed through the trees. Something made her stop and look upward, and she felt suddenly as if she were being watched.

She looked back down the trail and sniffed the breeze that ruffled her fur. No one was behind her. After waiting for a moment, she lowered her head and went on.

A rustle in the branches overhead stopped her again and she peered suspiciously up into the canopy. A small brown head with a banded muzzle appeared through the leaves a short distance above her head. It stared at her with round black eyes.

"Aree?" it said.

Ratha stared back. Her mouth opened and her jaw sagged until she was gaping. "Aree? Have I really found you?"

The treeling yawned at her and scratched himself. He leaned down to peer at Ratha, extending his long ringed tail for balance. Then, as if satisfied, he ambled along the branch and climbed down into the crotch of the tree.

At first Ratha thought she had made a mistake. This creature was a bit larger and considerably rounder than Thakur's treeling. Then she saw the crooked rear leg.

Unless another treeling had also managed to break its leg in exactly the same place, this one had to be Aree.

Ratha talked softly to the treeling, trying to coax him down, but Aree seemed shy and unsure. He would start to climb down, then hesitate and scramble back up to his perch.

"Come on, Aree. You know who I am. You used to groom my fur. It needs grooming now," she said and started to purr.

Aree was never afraid of me once he got used to me. He used to jump all over me. I wonder what has made him so shy.

The treeling started to groom himself, nuzzling the bulge of his belly. *His?* Aree was obviously a female and had found a mate.

"Thakur will have to get used to thinking of you as a she," Ratha said, grinning. "He'll also have to get used to all your little cubs, when you have them."

Aree cocked her head and curled her tail at Ratha, but wouldn't budge from the tree no matter how loud she purred. Ratha was starting to worry when she remembered the command Thakur had used to call the treeling to him.

She drew in her breath, gave a short hiss and clicked her teeth twice. Aree's eyes brightened. The treeling launched herself from the tree, bounced to the ground and then up onto Ratha's back. She rubbed her cheek against Ratha and was answered with nuzzles and licks. The creature took her place on Ratha's shoulder and wound her tail around Ratha's neck.

When she was sure Aree would stay on her back, she turned around and trotted down the trail to the meadow, eager to find Thakur.

As she drew close and heard the sound of cubs' voices,

she hesitated. Carrying Aree out into the open sun of the meadow might not be the best idea. If Thakur's young pupils saw her with the treeling on her back, they would crowd around her with eager curiosity and might frighten Aree. If the treeling panicked and ran away, she would never be able to get her back again.

She left the trail before it led into the meadow and circled through the brush at the edge of the grass until she reached a leafy thicket. Here she was close enough to see and hear everything. The wind blew toward her and she caught the sweaty smell of dapplebacks and the eager nervous scents of the youngsters.

The cubs were watching as Thakur chased two dapplebacks across the meadow. The horses pounded in front of him, their manes flying. He raced after them, lithe and slim, yet powerful. With a sudden burst of speed, he caught up with the dapplebacks and dashed between them. It seemed as though he drove right under those flying heels, and Ratha forgot to breathe until she saw the horses separate with Thakur running between them.

The cubs also stood transfixed and Ratha imagined they were doubting whether they would ever be able to cut and drive dapplebacks the way he did. As a herder in training, she had practiced endlessly before she could attempt what he had just done. An instant of indecision or a false step could bring the herder down to be trampled beneath those sharp-toed feet.

Ratha saw Thakur jog to a stop. Ahead of him, the two horses slowed, grunting and snorting. These dapplebacks were more lively than the old mare he had been using; she guessed the cubs had reached a stage in their training where they could work a beast with more spirit.

Aree shifted on her back, reminding her why she had

come here. She looked for the nearest cub and recognized Fessran's younger son who was standing in the sparse shade near the edge of the grass.

"Sst! Khushi!" Ratha called, leaning out of her hiding place. The cub jumped and turned his head back over his shoulder.

"Sst! Over here. Quickly."

Khushi blinked as he caught sight of her. With a quick look to either side, he galloped over to her thicket.

"Clan leader!" he said, his eyes large with surprise. "What are you doing, hiding in the bushes?"

"Never mind that," she said, trying to keep enough leaves over her head to conceal the treeling. "Go get your teacher. Tell him that I have something for him."

Khushi eyed her doubtfully. "Clan leader, he's really grumpy today. If I interrupt him, he'll chew my ears and they're already pretty ragged."

"I have something for him that will help his temper," she answered. At that instant Aree chose to poke her head through the leaves and Khushi's eyes got bigger than ever. "Oooh!"

Ratha ducked farther back in the thicket. "I've got Thakur's lost friend. Hurry up and get him, or *I'll* chew your ears!"

With a gasp, Khushi took off and scampered across the grass to where Thakur was supervising the other cubs as they rounded up the two dapplebacks. Khushi had to tug at Thakur's tail to get the herding teacher's attention and Ratha saw him duck an irritated swipe. But the cub was persistent and at last Thakur left his pupils with the dapplebacks and crossed the grass to Ratha's hiding place.

"Ratha?" he called crossly. "Khushi said you were here. Where . . . ?"

She was lifting her foot over a low branch when Aree gave a joyful squeal and sprang over her head. She had forgotten to unwind her tail completely from around Ratha's neck. Suddenly unbalanced, Ratha spilled out onto the grass and landed on her front.

She looked up, dazed and half-choked. Aree hung between the two of them, suspended by the tail, with her arms around Thakur's neck. She was rubbing her cheek against his and cooing as if she would never stop. Thakur looked as taken aback as Ratha was. His jaw sagged open against the treeling's arm and he stared at Ratha in complete bewilderment for an instant.

Then his drooping whiskers sprang up and his ears perked. His disbelief quickly gave way to delight.

"Aree!" he cried as the treeling loosed her tail from Ratha's neck and hugged him with her legs and arms. "Aree, you're really back! Oh how I've missed you, you little flea-picker! You can eat fruit on my back all day long and dribble and I'll never complain, just as long as you stay."

Ratha picked herself up and smoothed the rumpled fur on her breast. "And not a word of thanks to the brave clan leader who risked paws and tail to bring this unpredictable creature back to you?" she said hoarsely, adding a cough for effect.

"He didn't hurt you badly, did he?" Thakur asked, wrinkling the fur on his brow. She sat up stiffly. *"She"*— Ratha paused—"nearly choked me to death. The next time you lose your treeling, the clan may need another leader."

Thakur eyed Aree with astonishment. "You're right. He's a she and soon there will be more of them."

"If Aree's cubs prove to be as clever as she is, then

we've solved Fessran's problem, haven't we?" Ratha grinned at Thakur.

"If I can train all her young ones. I don't know how I'm going to teach herding and cope with a whole treeling family at the same time," he added with mild dismay.

"When the time comes, I'll help you," Ratha offered. Then she explained how she had found the treeling, and how the creature had stayed in the tree until she hissed and clicked her teeth. "I don't know why Aree was so afraid of me. She used to enjoy grooming my fur," she said, puzzled.

Thakur had been nosing the treeling and licking her coat. He paused, went back over a spot he had licked before and carefully spread the treeling's fur with his tongue and teeth.

"Look," he said, his voice indistinct. Ratha peered at Aree's back. On the treeling's skin she saw two bright pink lines side by side. They were half-healed claw marks.

"Now we know that she didn't just run off on her own," Ratha said at last. "Someone chased her."

"And nearly caught her," Thakur added, his voice grim. Aree shook herself and smoothed her fur. "You were too fast for Shongshar, weren't you, little tree-climber?"

"So you think it was Shongshar," she said in a low voice.

"Yes. There is no one else who had as good a reason for getting rid of Aree. He's convinced that the only way to master the Red Tongue is by strength and fierceness. My Aree proved that there is another way. If the Fire-keepers listen to me, they will no longer believe Fessran and Shongshar. Fessran might be willing to change, but not Shongshar."

"What about Bundi's accident?" Ratha asked.

Thakur's eyes narrowed. "That is harder to explain. Shongshar and Bundi were like lair-brothers. Even now, I find it difficult to believe that he could deliberately hurt Bundi."

"I found his pawprints at the edge of the firebed," Ratha told him.

"That doesn't prove anything. Shongshar could have been there earlier, helping to light the fire. No. I think it was Nyang who pushed Bundi."

"Fessran's son?" Ratha was startled by this suggestion, but the more she thought about it, the more it made sense. "Yes. Nyang would do anything to please Shongshar. I have seen how that cub looks at him."

"Yes, but we don't have any evidence," Thakur reminded her.

"You know me too well, herding teacher," Ratha said, somewhat ruefully. "Until I can prove to myself that Shongshar and Nyang are guilty, I can't punish them. If they are, they have covered their tracks well."

"And you may not be able to unbury those tracks. I think we should look ahead on this trail, not back," said Thakur. "Now that Aree has returned, we can continue training her with the fire."

Ratha felt a slight twinge of uncertainty. "Do you think that's really a good idea? I mean . . ." She faltered as he stared at her in surprise. "We aren't sure what happened to Bundi, are we? It might have been the fire-creature itself that burned him."

"Don't tell me that you've been listening to that dapple-back dung! It may be fit for frightening litterlings, but you have more sense."

She hesitated, thinking about her dream. "I know, but sometimes I'm not sure. What happened to Bundi scared me."

"It frightened others too. If Fessran had posted a Fire-keeper to guard the herders' fire before Bundi's accident, the yowls would have set her fur on end. Now no one complains."

"They're glad," said Ratha. "That also frightens me a little. I'm not sure what to do."

"Help me work with the treelings," Thakur suggested. "We can continue teaching Aree, and after her little ones are born, we can train them too."

"Then Fessran won't worry about having only one treeling," said Ratha excitedly. "She may even decide to help us."

"Maybe later, but for now we should keep this as secret as we can," Thakur cautioned.

"Bring Aree to my den this evening, then. I'll have a fire there. If we keep the Red Tongue small, it won't be able to hurt her."

"I will. I have to get back to my pupils now," he added, glancing over to where several cubs stood watching him with their tails raised in curiosity.

Ratha stayed hidden long enough to be sure that Thakur could manage both Aree and the rambunctious cubs. When she was satisfied that he was in no danger of losing the creature again, she slipped away.

She decided to go and inspect the ground near Thakur's den for any traces of footprints. The old ashes from the last fire Bira had built for him were still there and the site had been left alone. She might find some faint prints she had overlooked before.

On her way along the path that wound through scattered trees, she heard far-off splintering sounds and cracks. Soon a Firekeeper came hurrying along the trail, with kindling in his mouth. The sounds of breaking wood continued and another Firekeeper followed with a jagged piece of a dead log that he could barely get his jaws around.

Ratha looked after him with mild curiosity. Her interest became stronger when a third wood-carrier followed. As he disappeared, she heard the footsteps of yet another. Bira appeared with a mouthful of fragrant pine twigs. As she approached she ducked her head respectfully to Ratha, which made her drop several sticks. When she tried to retrieve them, she only lost more. She attempted to snag them with her claws and push them into her mouth with her pads, but finally she lost patience and unloaded the whole mouthful.

"I shouldn't try to carry so many at once," she said, spitting out pieces of gray bark, "but Fessran wanted us to hurry."

"Where are you taking it?" asked Ratha. She gathered up some of the scattered twigs and placed them beside Bira's pile of sticks.

"Oh, the wood isn't for a gathering fire," Bira said quickly. "Fessran's found a cave beside the waterfall and we're putting wood in there so it will stay dry during the rainy season."

Ratha helped Bira get all the twigs secured between her teeth and the young Firekeeper trotted away with a grateful wave of her tail.

Ratha stared up the path, thinking. Fessran hadn't told her about a cave for storing wood. It sounded sensible enough, although there was no need to hurry; the rainy season wouldn't start for a long time. *I think I'll just follow Bira up there and look around.*

She took the same trail she had taken that morning and soon passed the place where she had found Aree. She saw that her pugmarks had been wiped away under the feet of the Firekeepers who had passed this way. A stray pine twig told her that Bira hadn't managed to hold onto all her load.

She wondered how long they had been doing this and whether they had stopped when she took the path earlier. She had noticed that the trail beside the creek looked a little more worn than usual, and there were more smells about.

The creek trail ran between great trees whose charred rough bark spoke of the Red Tongue's passing. Farther on, the path wound around outcroppings of coarse-grained stone that had weathered and crumbled to form a white gravel that crunched beneath her pads. The grade became steep, and by the time she reached the huge granite slab that lay at the base of the waterfall, she was panting slightly.

Ratha stood, letting the wind-blown spray cool her as she studied the tumbled boulders near the foot of the cliff. She tensed as something moved in the shadows. It took form, becoming a head and forelegs. A Firekeeper emerged from a cleft between the rocks. He was so intent on his work that he did not see her, and he soon disappeared out of sight down the trail she had just climbed up.

She threaded her way through the scattered rockfalls until she reached the cleft. She was about to enter when she heard voices echoing inside. Quickly she backed off. One of the voices was Fessran's. The other, louder one was Shongshar's.

"I really think we should have told her before we started." Fessran sounded querulous. "It's obvious that this will benefit the rest of the clan, not just our Fire-keepers."

"And suppose she doesn't see it that way," Shongshar hissed, and the echo from the rock walls added menace to the voice that carried to Ratha. "Suppose she treats this as she has treated our gatherings, showing little respect for us and the fire-creature we serve."

"She won't, Shongshar. I . . ."

Fessran's voice faltered and Ratha knew a stray breeze had wafted her scent into the cavern. When the Fire-keeper leader came out her face had an odd, tight look as if she were angry but was afraid to lose her temper. Shong-shar followed her and fixed Ratha with his strange un-readable gaze. He had changed so much in the time since he had given up his witless young that she no longer knew what to expect from him.

"I was told you were storing wood up here," she said briskly, not looking at either one of them. "That is a good idea. I would like to see how much you have gathered."

"Not very much. Why don't you come back later when we have sorted and stacked it?" Fessran said, with a glance at Shongshar.

"Then show me the cave," Ratha said flatly, making sure they knew this was no longer a request.

Silently Shongshar turned his gray bulk around and led the way in. Ratha went after him and heard Fessran following. She expected to have to use her whiskers while her eyes adapted to the gloom, but she found that the low tunnel was lit by a faint wavering light.

Her ears caught a soft, steady roar that grew louder as they traveled farther into the cavern. The light grew stronger, making Shongshar into a gray-brown shadow ahead of her and tinting Fessran's eyes with a ruddy glow.

The sound grew louder still. Ratha, following Shong-shar, found herself in a larger cave whose roof arched away into shadow. Crystal-flecked pillars reflected the fierce orange light from the fire that burned in the center of the cavern.

Ratha felt her fur rise. She had been in caves before, but they had been lighted only by the soft phosphorescence of slimy plants that grew on their walls. She had sensed the vastness and emptiness of those underground caverns only by the echoes that reached her ears or by the clammy breeze that seemed to come from the depths of the earth. Now, with the fire's light, she could examine an entire chamber.

Pillars of rough limestone reared up until they were lost in the shadows that played on the roof of the cave. Fang-shaped stones rose from the floor to guard the entrances to other chambers deeper in the rock, whose ageless emptiness seemed to seep into the cave in which she stood.

She looked around in awe, feeling small and fearful amid the ominous majesty of the great cavern. Against the base of a pillar, the Firekeepers had begun piling kindling. The wood looked untidy and out of place against the fire-jeweled pillar. There were a few Firekeepers in the rear of the chamber; Ratha had not noticed them at first, since they blended into the moving shadows cast by the Red Tongue.

The cave itself was not the only awesome thing. Ratha felt her gaze drawn almost unwillingly to the fire. Its sound filled the chamber and its light danced on the pillars and the walls. Here, its presence was overwhelming and shadowed everything else. Here, its power was contained and strengthened. Here was a place where the Red Tongue ruled.

Again Ratha remembered her dream, and she could almost see the coal-red eyes of the dream creature forming in the fire's heart. She fought fear with anger, turning suddenly on Fessran.

"Why have you brought the fire in here?" she demanded. "I thought this was to serve only as a place for keeping wood."

It was not Fessran but Shongshar who answered. "Our Firekeepers find it difficult to see when they come in from daylight. We have lighted the cave so they can see where to place their wood. Surely you see the sense in doing so, clan leader."

Despite herself, Ratha had to agree that his reason was valid. She felt frustrated at being unable to find an explanation for the sense of uneasiness that clawed at her belly. She asked more questions, but the answers all made sense, even though they didn't satisfy her. Why had they picked such a large cavern? The smaller ones were above the falls and more difficult to reach. Why hadn't they built the fire in the less spacious gallery that led to the cave? It was too damp and the wood must be kept dry.

At last Ratha said, "When you are finished gathering wood, you will no longer need the fire-creature in the cave. I want it taken out."

"We will need it here when the rainy season comes," Fessran protested.

"I will decide what to do when the rainy season comes. When you are finished stacking wood, you will take the Red Tongue out of here."

"As you wish, clan leader," Shongshar said in a low

growl. Fessran looked as if she wanted to say something else, but remained silent.

Ratha found her way out of the cave. The bright day hurt her eyes, but she was suddenly grateful for the sunlight and blue sky. She breathed air made crisp by spray from the falls, shook herself and went back down the trail.

The task of wood gathering took much more time than Ratha expected. Once or twice she nearly lost her temper, but Fessran pointed out that if she wanted the herds to be safely guarded, the Firekeepers had to have dry fodder for the guard-fires. Ratha remembered the bristlemane attack and reluctantly agreed to let the Firekeepers finish their task.

Although she disliked being in the cave, she went up to it every once in a while to see how the Firekeepers were doing. On her most recent trip, she noticed that Fessran had set someone outside to guard the cavern entrance.

This made her more uneasy than ever. As soon as enough wood was stockpiled for the rainy season, she was going to put a stop to the activity in the cave.

CHAPTER 14

THE TASK OF GATHERING WOOD continued to go slowly and Ratha's impatience grew. Each day that the fire burned in the cave seemed to add to the strength and influence of the Firekeepers. Every day that she was in the meadow, she would hear the herders talking about the cave-den of the Red Tongue. Some were bold enough to speak about visiting it, although none of them had, as far as she knew.

Midsummer passed and the green of the meadow grass turned to pale gold. The herdbeasts coughed in the dust raised by the dry wind. The little stream that flowed through the meadow shrank to a trickle and the herders began taking the animals to the river to water. The Firekeepers took great care in clearing the places where the guard-fires were lit, for a single spark could set the meadow aflame.

The Firekeepers' task began drawing to an end at last. Even Fessran agreed with Ratha that enough dry wood had been stored to last through the longest rainy season. She was less agreeable about taking the Red Tongue out of the cave, and Ratha found, to her dismay, that not only the Firekeepers, but many of the herders wanted it kept there. Why protect only the Red Tongue's food from the wind and rain? Did it make sense to do that while the fires that were the main source for lighting all the others were left ill-protected in shallow dens dug for them in the meadow? In a bad storm, the fire-lairs could flood. Why not keep a source-fire safe in the deep cave? Then the clan would never have to worry about losing the Red Tongue even in the fiercest of storms.

What angered Ratha most about this idea was that she had no good reason to reject it. The bristlemane attack during a rainstorm had showed her how vulnerable the herds could be if the Red Tongue failed. The argument was simple and obvious. At times she could almost convince herself to think about it that way.

But the shadow of her dream remained in her mind. She still saw the hunger of those coal-red eyes and heard the voice that was the rush of the flames. "Bare your throat to me, for I am the one who rules," it had said and her terror had made her crouch and tremble, lifting her chin. Others of the Named would do so more willingly and knowing that frightened her in a way she could not understand.

Her belly knew the truth of her fear, but her tongue had no words to shape it. How could she hold the image of her dream-creature up before the clan as a reason to reject something that might be essential to the clan's survival? She wondered if the danger she saw was only an illusion; that she was growing fainthearted and unwilling to take risks.

The heat of the afternoon lay heavily on her as she padded along the trail that led to Thakur's den. She smelled the scent of summer leaves and of faded flowers whose centers were swelling into fruit. Once she would have stopped to let the smells fill her nose with the richness of the season, but now her cares pushed aside any enjoyment.

She found Thakur lying in the shade outside his lair. Aree was not perched in her usual place on his shoulder. She sat huddled up against him. As Ratha approached, the treeling tried to curl herself up, but her pregnant belly kept her from doing much more than looping her long tail over her shoulder. She seemed restless and unable to get comfortable.

Ratha was so used to seeing Aree on Thakur's back or the nape of his neck that the treeling looked odd sitting beside him.

Thakur caught her look. He raised his head and grinned

at her. "Poor flea-picker is getting too bulgy to stay on my shoulder. She wobbled a lot this morning and I thought she was going to tumble off."

"When will she have her cubs?"

"Tonight, I think. She's been gathering fern leaves for a nest in the back of my lair and her smell has changed."

Aree reached up on Thakur's flank, grasped two handfuls of fur and heaved herself up onto him. She reached for his tail, which he obligingly curled across his leg where she could reach it. She began pulling out tufts of hair and bundled them together in her fingers.

"She found out I was still shedding a little and she likes the fur to line her nest," Thakur explained.

"I hope she leaves you enough to cover your tail," Ratha observed, as the treeling pulled out a large tuft of his fur.

"Ouch!" Thakur flicked his tail out of Aree's reach. "All right, you've got plenty. You'd better go build your nest before you decide to have your cubs on top of me."

"*Aree!*" agreed the treeling as she clambered off him and shuffled into the den, holding the wad of fur.

Thakur looked after her anxiously for a minute. "I'm glad you came," he said to Ratha. "You know more about this than I do."

"Me? I don't know anything about treelings," she protested.

"Yes, but you do know about having cubs."

Ratha cocked her head at him. "I did it once. I don't see how that is going to help."

"Well, maybe not," Thakur conceded. "At least you can tell me what she's doing."

Ratha expected that Aree would soon emerge from the

den to gather more leaves or steal more fur. As the afternoon shadows lengthened and the treeling didn't appear, Thakur began to get nervous.

"Maybe I should go and see if she's all right," he said, rolling to his feet. He crept inside until only his tail hung out. "She's in the nest, on her side," he called, his voice muffled. "She's moving a little and making funny noises."

Ratha poked her head in alongside his flank and listened. She could hear Aree breathing and every few breaths the treeling gave a soft grunt. Satisfied that everything sounded all right, Ratha withdrew from the lair and gave a tug on Thakur's tail.

"Come out, herding teacher. You're worse than a curious yearling at birthing time. The best thing you can do now is leave her alone."

Thakur backed out of the den, his fur rumpled. "Anyone would think *you* had sired Aree's cubs," Ratha teased.

"Don't hold it against me, clan leader," he said wryly. "After all, this may be as close as I get to having a family of my own."

She winced. "I'm sorry, Thakur. I didn't mean to remind you."

"Don't be. I've become used to living with it," he said. "I decided not to take the chance and, after seeing what happened to Shongshar's cubs, I'm more convinced than ever." He paused. "I don't think you would want to have to abandon another litter, especially if I was their father."

She stretched out with her hindquarters in the sun and the rest of her in the dappled shade. She laid her head on her paws and felt grateful to Thakur that he had the sensitivity to make himself absent during the time the females were in heat. By doing so, he freed her from having to make the painful decision: whether to exile him during the mating season or allow him to take a partner. She sighed. If only Shongshar had done the same!

"Thakur," she said suddenly. "Do you think Shongshar's cubs are still alive?"

It was a while before he answered. "I don't think so. Why?"

"I wonder if I should have told him we didn't kill them. If I had let him know where we left them, he might have been able to go and see them." She lifted her head. "I didn't tell him because I thought he might try to bring them back. Perhaps it would have been better had I trusted him." She fell silent awhile and then asked softly, "Do you think it would do any good to tell him now?"

"No," Thakur answered. "If there was a time that it would have done any good, that time is past. His grief has set him on a new trail and he has been on it too long."

She sighed. "I wish I knew why Fessran listens to him."

"She listens to him for the same reason you find it difficult to disbelieve his words: he understands the power of the Red Tongue and he knows how to use it."

"I don't know whether they are his words or Fessran's. All I know is that they give me a feeling in my belly that I don't like and I can't do anything about it."

He leaned closer, listening, and she felt her despair rising up again. "He is so clever! Everything he says or tells Fessran to say makes sense. He is right about sheltering the Red Tongue in the cave during the winter rains. He seems to think only of the safety of my people, but my belly tells me he has other reasons for what he does."

"Your belly has been right before," said Thakur.

"Yes, but my belly only had to persuade the rest of

me that it was right. Persuading others is harder," Ratha grumbled.

Thakur shifted so that he was farther into the sun and half-closed his eyes. Ratha was afraid he was going to drift off to sleep, but he opened his eyes and said, "The important thing is to show Fessran what treelings can do. She will see that there is another way to make use of the Red Tongue's power. I think she listens to Shongshar because she thinks there is no way other than his."

"Now that we will soon have more treelings, there is another way. I know we still have to train them and there may still be problems, but I think it will work." She was about to say more when Thakur sat up and looked intently toward the lair.

"I hear Aree," he said. "I think she wants me."

Despite Ratha's admonitions, he entered the den. She could only sigh and follow. When her eyes became accustomed to the dimness, she saw Thakur curled around the treeling's nest. How he had done so without disturbing her, Ratha didn't know, but Aree seemed to be pleased that he was there. The treeling wriggled herself close to him. He began to purr and she crooned softly to herself.

The blend of sounds soothed Ratha and made her drowsy. She laid her cheek against the hard-packed soil of the den floor and let herself drift. She was within the earth, as she had been in the Red Tongue's cave, but here she felt sheltered and safe rather than afraid.

Daylight faded outside, but the moon rose, and she could see by the faint silvery light that filtered into the den. Aree grew restless again and Ratha heard her turning about inside her nest. Thakur's half-closed eyes opened wide. Aree halted, crouched and seemed to shudder. She gave a deep grunt, a noise Ratha had never heard from a treeling before. She grunted again and began to pant.

"She's pushing at me with her feet," Thakur said. "Do you think she's all right?"

"Yes. I made all sorts of strange noises when I was birthing my cubs. Let her push against you if she needs to."

Ratha's curiosity was suddenly overwhelmed by a sense of joyous excitement. This was the way she had felt when she knew that her first cub was pushing its way out from within her. Even the later knowledge that her litterlings were no more than animals couldn't mar this first memory, and it came flooding back to her so that she began to pant eagerly along with Aree. It did not matter that these were treeling cubs rather than those of the Named; the wonder was still the same.

"Anyone would think *you* were birthing these litterlings," Thakur teased gently.

Too excited to feel abashed, she peered into the nest, trying to see as much as she could. Aree gave an odd sort of heave and made a long grunt that was almost a growl.

"The first one's coming, Thakur!" Ratha hissed. She heard Aree take a deep breath and growl again, and then there was something else in the nest, a shiny wriggling bundle that made tiny noises of its own. She saw the treeling's eyes glint as the little mother curled around to lick her firstborn and free it from the birth-cord that still bound it to her body.

Ratha remembered the taste and feel of salty wet fur on her own tongue and the way the tiny thing mewed and writhed beneath her muzzle. She heard a surprisingly strong cry and then fast snuffling sounds as the newborn creature began to breathe.

Aree gathered her litterling to her and nursed it. She ate the afterbirth that soon followed and began to grunt again. The second treeling cub quickly followed its elder sibling and Aree lay against Thakur, cradling both little ones in her arms.

Several more arrived in the nest and Aree had to lie on her side to nurse them.

"I think she's finished," said Thakur after they had waited a long time for more treeling cubs to appear.

"I'm not surprised. Her litter is larger than any of ours."

"How many are there?" asked Thakur. "I can't see them all."

"She has as many litterlings as you have paws," said Ratha.

"That's a clever way to think about it," said Thakur, admiringly. "Whenever I want to know if I have all my herdbeasts together, I just smell them and I know which smells are missing. But we don't know the treelings' smells very well yet."

"Until we do, just match them up with your paws. If you have a paw left over, then you know a little treeling is missing."

She saw Thakur's outline against the faintly moonlit wall of the den as he leaned over to nose his treeling. "Aree certainly doesn't care how many there are. She's happy."

The sound of the treeling's crooning filled the den. Soon Thakur joined in with a deep purr and Ratha found herself adding her own note. She wasn't sure when his purr faded, for soon afterward, her own voice fell silent and she joined him in sleep.

It seemed that she had just closed her eyes when she was awakened by a nudge in the ribs. She rolled onto her back and blinked sleepily at Thakur. Brilliant morning sunlight lit the floor of the den near the entrance and the growing warmth promised a hot day.

"I have to go and teach my pupils, Ratha," he said as he stepped over her, trailing his shadow. "Can you watch Aree and her litterlings until I get back?"

She yawned and shook her pelt, trying to rid herself of the sleepiness that still clung to her. She remembered the previous night's events and came fully awake.

"How is Aree doing?" she asked.

"She just fed her litterlings again and they're all asleep. They're so tiny, but they already look fat."

Ratha peered into the nest at the four balls of damp-fluffed fur curled up against the larger lump that was their mother. For a while, she lay with her chin resting on her crossed forepaws and watched the treelings sleep.

Later, she went outside to stretch her legs and keep watch. When she went in again to escape the full strength of the noon sun, she found Aree was awake and nursing two of her young while the others slept. She alternately dozed and watched the treeling family. Sometimes Aree would lie on her side and feed her little ones in the same manner as did the females of the Named. But often she nursed them in a different way, cradling them in her arms and holding them to her teats.

Ratha found this strange and endlessly fascinating. Aree seemed to know how to exchange her youngsters so that all got an equal share of milk, rather than having to fight their littermates for it as did the cubs of the Named. She became so absorbed that she didn't notice the afternoon was passing until she smelled Thakur and heard his footsteps outside the den.

She was almost reluctant to give him back the duty of

watching the treelings, but she also felt slightly guilty for hiding away where no one could find her.

Promising to return and look after the treelings the following morning, she gave Thakur a farewell nuzzle and trotted away. She took the trail leading back to the meadow and soon heard footsteps coming from the other direction. Ratha saw one of the herders approaching her. His steps were quick and purposeful, his eyes strangely intent, as if he were looking at something that always floated ahead of him.

A look of startled surprise came over his face. He ducked his head as he passed Ratha, but he did not slow his pace. She stopped and watched his hindquarters disappear around a bush.

He certainly didn't expect to see me, thought Ratha. His astonishment had been tinged with a look of shame, as if she had caught him doing something forbidden and she knew at once he was on his way to the Red Tongue's cave.

She wanted to race down the path after him and order him back to the meadow. That thought quickly gave way to a feeling of frustration. He knew exactly what he was doing. The look on his face told her that. Even if she caught him and scolded him, he would probably do it again.

She decided instead to follow him at a distance and watch what happened when he arrived at the cave. His scent was fresh and his trail easy to follow. She thought he might already be within the cave as she crept up the last stretch of the trail, but she heard his voice over the sound of the waterfall.

She hid herself in the scattered boulders to the side of the path and peered over, pricking her ears as far forward as they would go. The herder had his back to her so that she could see only his tail, which had begun to curl and wag. The cool breeze from the falls carried the scent of his dismay and another, less pleasant smell, the smug self-satisfaction of the two Firekeepers who barred his way.

"This is the Red Tongue's den, not a place to amuse idle dappleback-keepers," one of them growled.

"Just let me in for a little while. You speak so much of the strength and beauty of the fire-creature within this cave that I want to see it for myself."

"Perhaps you think yourself worthy to serve it, young herder." The other Firekeeper grinned. "I see you bothered to groom the manure out of your fur before you came, so the Red Tongue won't be too displeased."

The herder's tail sprang upright and he took an eager step toward the cleft in the rocks. Again the Firekeepers blocked him.

"Not so quickly, dung-wearer," the larger one snapped. "First we must tell you what you may or may not do when you are inside."

"All right, tell me." The herder turned his ears slightly back.

"Keep your ears up and your tail down. No scratching or licking."

"I scratch myself near the guard-fires," said the herder, mystified.

"Well, you shouldn't. And this is different. This is the Red Tongue's den and you should be respectful. Are you ready?"

The herder answered that he was. One Firekeeper led him in while the other stayed beside the entrance. He wasn't gone long before he was led out again, but Ratha could tell he was dazed and awestruck. He blinked and, as he looked at the Firekeepers, a new, envious hunger came into his eyes.

"You must have been judged most worthy to serve such a wondrous creature," he said, and Ratha could see that his words inflated their pride even further. She was tempted to jump out from her hiding place and snarl at them for being so supercilious and overbearing, but she held herself back. She needed to learn more before she could confront Fessran and Shongshar with any real proof of wrongdoing among the Firekeepers.

She decided to come back and hide herself again the following day to gather more evidence. If the behavior of these two Firekeepers was any indication, she thought sourly, she would soon have all she needed. Perhaps she could even persuade Fessran to hide and listen, for she sensed that the Firekeeper leader was growing uneasy about her dependence on Shongshar and her toleration of his methods.

During the next few days, Ratha fell into a regular routine of watching Thakur's treelings while he was gone in the morning and then hiding out near the fire-cave and observing what went on there. More herders came to visit. Some, like Cherfan, she liked and respected, and it dismayed her that they were drawn here. At first the herders came to satisfy their curiosity, but their interest soon became fascination and they returned again and again to enter the cave.

Ratha noticed that the Firekeepers became more selective about whom they would admit. Herders who were eager to crouch before the fire-creature had to obey rules that seemed to grow harsher and more arbitrary each time

Ratha listened to them. She ground her teeth and growled —promising herself that once Fessran understood what was happening she would end these abuses.

Yet, the more she watched, the more uncertain she became. Those who came to the cave begged to enter with such unabashed eagerness that Ratha felt shame for them. They were blind to the pettiness of the Firekeepers' rules, accepting these restrictions as part of the ritual that seemed to be growing up around the cave.

As she watched, she gained a new and disconcerting knowledge of her people. There was something in the nature of the Named that drove them to crouch in obedience to this new power. Ratha sensed in them a confusion of loyalties. Never before had she thought her position as clan leader might be seriously threatened. She was the one who had brought this new power to the clan. She had tamed the Red Tongue and driven the Un-Named back in terror before its power. All the Named were grateful to her and all bared their throats to her.

But, she realized, they did not look upon her with the same awe and passion as they gave to the thing she had once called her creature. Without the blazing presence of a firebrand in her jaws, she had only the power of claws and teeth—and loyalty based on fading memories. Yes, she had tamed the Red Tongue, but she had given its keeping to others and been blind to how it changed them.

She began to see the real truth behind her dream. Her mind had built an image of a Named One made of fire to show her how deep its power reached within her people and even within herself.

"We are all crying cubs before it," Thakur had said once long ago. Ratha remembered his words and thought,

Once, I alone could stand before it without fear. Now I know I am no better than the others.

One day in late summer, she lay in her hiding place with the sun on her back and her chin on the rock, far enough from the Firekeeper guards so they wouldn't smell her. The air was still and even the sound of the fall seemed to be muffled by the heat. No one had come all afternoon and the two Firekeepers were dozing where they sat. Ratha was thinking about leaving her refuge to drink from the stream above the falls when she heard claws scraping on rock. She ducked down and peered through a cleft between two boulders. For a moment, the crack framed an ugly face with lop ears and bile-yellow eyes.

Shoman! What was he doing there?

Ratha saw his grizzled brown coat and his kinked tail as he passed her hiding place. Someone followed him, and she caught a glimpse of a burn-scarred muzzle and the faded spots of a yearling.

"Bundi?" she whispered to herself, but she didn't need his smell to know the injured herder. She felt a sense of betrayal, although she was not quite sure why. Perhaps she had assumed that one who had been wounded by the Red Tongue would never seek its presence again.

She saw Shoman and Bundi approach the Firekeeper guards. One of them was Fessran's son Nyang and he came forward to challenge the two herders who sought entry.

"Take yourselves back down the trail," Nyang said, flattening his ears at them. "The Red Tongue has marked you as unfit to enter its lair."

"Unfit because I bear this scar, or unfit because I see

only what is there and not what others would have me see?" growled Shoman.

Nyang's eyes narrowed. "The fire-creature can make you see whatever it wishes you to see. If you do not believe, why are you here?"

"Because of this!" Shoman thrust his scarred foreleg at Nyang. "Because the other herders see this and shun me. I have never been liked and I never expected to be, but to have them wrinkle their noses and look at me as if I were a diseased carcass full of blowflies . . . that I can't bear."

"And you are not afraid that one who angered the fire-creature once may anger it again?" asked Nyang.

"If it is clumsiness that angers it, then it may have me," Shoman spat. "I did nothing wrong, but the other herders won't believe it. I would rather risk its anger than to go back down to the meadow and be hissed at with contempt." He paused. Ratha could not see his face, but she knew he was glaring at Nyang. At last he said, "If you won't let both of us in, then take Bundi. He suffered much more from the Red Tongue's touch than I did, and he is too young to be spurned and made one apart."

Shoman's rough sympathy with Bundi startled Ratha, who had thought that he was too bitter and selfish to care much about anyone else. His words were wasted on Nyang, who looked at him coldly.

"I need a better reason than that," he said and then leered at Shoman.

The herder gave a deep growl that ended in a sigh. "I thought you might. Bundi"—he turned to the youngster behind him—"bring the meat I gave you."

It was a small piece and Bundi had hidden it in his

mouth, concealing the sight and smell from anyone else. He came forward and disgorged it in front of Nyang.

The sight of the chunk of torn flesh lying on the stone before the Firekeeper enraged Ratha and she had to fight to keep herself concealed. No one had the right to take meat from a herdbeast carcass unless they were feeding a nursing mother. All in the clan ate together and shared equally until their bellies were filled. Stealing or hoarding was a shameful act, and by the old laws of the Named, a clan leader could demand that the culprit bare his throat for a killing bite.

Nyang smelled the meat, looked to either side to be sure no one else was watching and then fastened his jaws in it. Ratha let him eat half before she left her hiding place and stepped out onto the trail. At the sound of her footsteps, Nyang started and the other two whirled around.

"That meat is forbidden, Firekeeper," Ratha said, lowering her head as the hair rose on the nape of her neck. Nyang tried to gulp down the rest of it, but he choked and dropped it as she showed her fangs at him. She turned to Bundi, who could not answer her accusing stare.

"The meat is mine," Shoman said in a harsh voice. "It is from my share."

"You know as well as I do that we eat from the carcass where it lies," said Ratha fiercely. "Your share or not, it is stolen, and I will not tolerate such a shameful thing among my people."

He looked back at her, half-ashamed, half-defiant. "Do you allow a good herder to be shunned and spat on just because he bears the scars from an accident that was not his fault? I am speaking of Bundi, clan leader, not myself."

"What good would it do him to enter this cave?" Ratha asked. "The Red Tongue does not heal its own wounds."

"It can heal the wounds that are made by malicious words. If Bundi and I enter the cave as if to seek forgiveness and emerge unharmed, and if this news is spread among the other herders, then we will not be treated as outcasts."

Ratha wanted to ask why they had not come to Cherfan or to her, but another thought stilled her question. If Shoman had come to her, she could have ordered that all who were shunning him and Bundi stop doing so, but while she might have put an end to their acts, she could not have changed the feelings that showed in their eyes. Shoman had taken the only action he could, despite the risk. He had done it for Bundi as well as himself, and that made Ratha respect him.

"All right," she said at last. "Nyang, take them into the cave." With a last hungry look at the meat, the Firekeeper led the two herders in.

She picked up the remains of the meat, holding it with the tips of her fangs as if the taste was rancid. She pushed past the other Firekeeper guard, who had been watching in astonishment, and entered the low gallery that led into the cave.

She halted in the flickering shadows to watch Shoman and Bundi approach the fire. Shoman stood still, but Bundi crouched before the flame, ducking his head so low that his whiskers swept the ground.

Beyond them, on a ledge in the darkness at the rear of the cave, sat Shongshar and behind him Fessran. Their eyes were fixed on Bundi and they seemed to brighten as the young herder raised his chin as if to bare his throat.

Ratha leaped over a row of stone fangs and began to

walk purposefully toward the ledge at the rear of the cave. Bundi halted in his supplication and crept away from the fire. If he had ignored her and bared his throat to the fire-creature, she knew she would have filled the cave with her roar, but she stayed silent and set her feet quietly.

Her path took her past the two herders. She stopped briefly, narrowing her eyes against the firelight and said, "Go now. I will make sure the others learn that you are no longer to be shunned."

When the two were gone, Ratha continued her walk toward the rear of the cave.

"Why do you enter the Red Tongue's den without permission from the ones who guard it?" Fessran's voice came from the ledge, sounding hollow and threatening, yet there was also an edge of fear in her words.

"Because I am the one who tamed the creature for you, Firekeeper," Ratha answered, looking up at the two on the ledge. "And I am growing tired of these cub-games. Call Nyang here."

"My son? What has he done to offend the clan leader?"

Ratha had dropped the meat she carried in order to speak clearly. Now she picked it up and tossed it in front of the ledge. Both Fessran and Shongshar came to the edge of their perch and peered down, smelling the raw flesh. Shongshar fixed his eyes on Ratha.

"Your son accepted that meat from the two herders who wished to enter the cave. It was stolen from a clan kill," she said.

"Then punish the herders," Shongshar growled. "It is they who have done wrong." Fessran's eyes grew wide.

"It is also wrong to accept meat that has been stolen

or to demand it in return for allowing in herders who would otherwise be unwelcome," Ratha hissed.

"I think you misunderstand the intent of the herders, clan leader," said Shongshar easily as he draped himself along the edge. The gesture was casual, but she could read the intent in his half-veiled eyes. He was larger and more powerful than she remembered and the shadows gave his orange eyes a strange hidden malevolence. She knew he saw how her eyes traveled along his body, registering his bulk and the powerful muscles of his neck and forelegs.

He shifted himself again and continued, "It is a long way down to the meadow, and some of us do not get the chance to eat as much as those who stay near the kills. If the herders try to even things out by bringing us some meat, I see nothing wrong with it."

"Nyang is always hungry," said Fessran, trying to sound motherly and indulgent. "He'll eat anything without thinking about where it came from."

"It is my responsibility to see that everyone has an equal share of a kill. Nyang gets no less than his share and frequently tries to take from others. There is no need for the herders to bring you meat. If you think this cave is too far from the meadow, move your wood somewhere else."

Fessran glanced at Shongshar, but although he was aware of her gaze, Ratha noticed he did not look back at her. "I'll talk to Nyang," Fessran said at last.

"You should talk to all your Firekeepers. Before I leave, let me remind you that I will not permit anyone to steal from a carcass or accept meat that has been stolen." She turned to leave and then looked back over her shoulder. "If I find that this has happened again, I will have this fire killed and the wood moved somewhere else. Do you understand me? Good."

She whirled around, trotted across the cave floor, down the gallery and out into the sunlight. She felt cleansed by her anger and pleased that she had finally confronted this thing that had been festering in her mind like the canker made by a tick burrowing into her flesh. She felt as though she had found it and nipped it out. But she knew as she traveled down the trail in the hazy sunlight of late afternoon that she hadn't yet gotten all of it.

CHAPTER 15

THE HERDERS continued to visit the Red Tongue's cave. Some did so openly; others were ashamed and furtive, sneaking up the trail through the shadows. Ratha knew she could do nothing to stop them, but she kept a careful watch to see that no meat was taken. Once or twice, she had read that intention in someone's eyes as they sank their teeth into a haunch of three-horn, but her look and the slight lift of her lip as she growled quickly dissuaded them.

Her suspicion and the growing ascendancy of the Fire-keepers over the herders poisoned the rough-and-tumble yet good-natured competition for places about a culled herdbeast. Ratha made sure that everyone received an adequate share, and there was in fact less inequality than there had been before. But everyone ate in a tense silence, punctuated only by the sound of tearing flesh.

Ratha found herself eating less, for the atmosphere around a kill made the meat seem to taste rancid and stick in her throat. Even the cubs were subdued; they rarely dived in to snatch a piece of meat as they had done before. Perhaps they had learned that such antics could result in a fierce bite or scratch rather than an easygoing cuff.

No more food was stolen, and Ratha became less obvious about her watchfulness, hoping that the event would be forgotten and the clan would go back to its old ways. This helped a little. There was more conversation at mealtimes and even some humor, but the unspoken distrust between the Firekeepers and the herders was an undercurrent of ill-feeling that kept everyone on edge.

A few days after the last cull, Ratha noticed that one of the three-horn fawns that had been born that spring was missing. She questioned the herders closely and had them search, but no sign of the animal was found. To lose a herdbeast without explanation was a dangerous precedent and she made it clear to the herders that it was not to happen again.

Sometimes she felt as if she was no longer walking among her own people, but among strangers whose puzzled, resentful glances made her feel strangely lost. She looked for the animal herself and did no better than the herders.

At last Cherfan told her that the fawn had been diseased. It died when the herd was driven to the river and the carcass had been buried there as it was unfit for food. She suspected this was told to placate her; she knew Cherfan and the others were growing tired of her suspicions. She gave up the search, finally deciding that trying to discover the animal's fate would cost too much resentment and further divide the clan.

She found herself turning more and more to Thakur and his family of treelings as a relief from the burden of her leadership. Each morning, when the herding teacher went off to instruct his pupils, she stayed at his den and watched over Aree and her young ones until he returned.

At first, when the youngsters were too small to leave the nest, Ratha found her task easy and pleasant. They would nurse and sleep, although sometimes Aree would take them out into the morning sun to creep about and stare at the world with wide eyes. Like cubs, they were intensely curious and aware of everything around them. Ratha knew, however, that their awareness was not like that of the Named.

As the treelings grew older, the differences between them began to show. The larger of the two males was placid and even-tempered, while his brother made up for his small size with a bullying aggressive nature. Both the little females of the litter were lively and inquisitive, although one sister was reckless, tending to shred the objects of her curiosity, while the other would gaze at flowers or insects without touching them. She seemed to know how to be gentle without needing to be taught.

At first, Ratha was attracted to the larger and bolder of the two sisters. The young treeling shared qualities she had herself and which she thought she might want in a companion. She was stronger and had a beautifully marked pelt and distinctive masking around her muzzle. She was also adventurous, having been the first to come out of the nest. Aree was forever having to seize her tail and yank her out of trouble.

Although Ratha enjoyed the bigger female's rough-and-tumble play, she often felt her gaze wandering to the smaller sister. The little female's fur was less rich in color and her markings more subdued, but her gentle nature seemed to feed Ratha's hunger for affection in a way that even Thakur's companionship could not. The little treeling could sense when Ratha was troubled and would come to cuddle against her before settling down to groom her fur.

She wasn't sure when she decided that the little treeling was to be her companion. Perhaps it was when Thakur noticed the growing friendship and in a teasing way began to call the youngster "Ratha's Aree." Since Ratha could think of nothing better, she finally accepted the name. It was easier for her to blend the two words into one, so after a while, she began to call the little treeling "Rath-aree."

The ripening season soon started, and Aree climbed trees eagerly to gather fruit. At first, the young treelings disdained this new food, but they were growing too big to nurse and the sweet smell began to tempt them. It was not long before they were eating fruit with as much gusto as their mother.

From birth, the young treelings knew fire. Its glow flickered on the wall of the den above their nest, and they became as used to the smell and sound as they were to their own mother. When the litter was old enough for Aree to leave them for long periods, Thakur again began to teach her how to care for the Red Tongue. Soon they had an audience of youngsters, who attended each teaching session and watched their mother's training with eager curiosity.

Both Thakur and Ratha welcomed this interest and

began to test the little creatures for evidence of Aree's ability. They did this carefully and gradually, using the same methods that Thakur had used with Aree. Like their mother, the youngsters quickly discovered that the Red Tongue's warmth could be strong enough to hurt, but if they were careful, they would not be injured.

Ratha feared that her little treeling, Ratharee, might be too timid to train as a fire-bearer. She was indeed more cautious than the others, but underneath her shyness was a certain streak of determination. Like her siblings, she wanted to imitate her mother's prowess, and Ratha nuzzled her and praised her each time she made an effort to overcome her reticence.

Once it was evident that Aree's youngsters could be taught the same skills as their mother, Thakur and Ratha began to devote more teaching time to them. She found that he was a much better teacher than she, for he had the experience and the patience to repeat commands and actions endlessly until the pupil finally accepted and understood. Her own impatience often made her blunder, and she struggled hard to control it. Gradually she found herself more able to master her temper, especially with her own treeling Ratharee. The affection she felt for her little companion helped to keep her sense of urgency in check.

Urgency? Yes. Neither Ratha nor Thakur said it aloud, but both shared a feeling that training the treelings was important. How quickly it was done might affect what happened in the days to come. Fessran's old objection to depending on Aree alone was valid, but now that they had five treelings, the risk was much less. Thakur's continued training had made Aree herself much more dependable and less likely to do something unexpected,

such as the antics she had performed around the Firekeepers. But Ratha did have to grin when she remembered
the expressions on the faces of the torchbearers.

Surely when Fessran saw that Aree and her youngsters
could do, she would accept their services. Perhaps she
would choose a treeling for herself, although Thakur
might be reluctant to give one to Shongshar.

Aree was ready. Now all that remained was to get Fessran to bring the Firekeepers down for another demonstration, Ratha thought, but she found that doing so was
harder than she had anticipated. The Firekeeper leader
spent most of her time in the cave by the falls, watching
those who came to pay homage to the Red Tongue.
Shongshar was always with her, and in his presence she
seemed to change, becoming haughty and imperious. Yet
Ratha often caught a sudden look of misery on her face,
as if she sensed the effect he had on her.

He never seemed to let her out of his sight, accompany-
ing her down to the meadow to eat or going with her to
give orders to those who built the guard-fires. Recently,
he had begun to interrupt her or answer for her when
she spoke to anyone else, although he still treated her
with a deference that seemed exaggerated and sometimes
strangely sinister. It was difficult to get Fessran alone and,
even then, she seemed ill-at-ease and unwilling to talk.

Ratha finally bullied her away from Shongshar long
enough to get her to agree to see Aree's new skills. But
Fessran was deliberately vague about when the meeting
would take place. At last, Ratha could wait no longer.
She sent word by the Firekeeper Bira that Thakur would
set up a demonstration for the evening of the following
day. She built a fire near his den at sunset and selected the
best pine sticks for the treelings to use as torches. Thakur

drilled Aree one more time and then they settled down to wait.

The night had grown cold and the fire fallen low before Ratha admitted to herself that Fessran wasn't going to come. She stopped her angry pacing and let Ratharee climb down from her back.

"I'm going up to the cave," she said, staring out of the circle of firelight to where the path led away from Thakur's lair.

"I don't think that would be wise, Ratha," he said softly.

"Fessran will not disobey me when she looks into my eyes. I am tired of sidelong looks and all this sneaking around."

"Then let me come with you. The trail can be treacherous at night."

"The only treachery is within that den of belly-crawlers," Ratha growled. "No, you stay here with Aree and her little ones. Keep the fire going until I return with Fessran. I won't be gone long."

She heard him sigh and turn away, but she was too angry for his words to hold her back, or even to think that her hasty actions might place him in danger.

She leaped away into the night, her rage giving her speed. There was no moon that night and the trees that overhung the creek trail made the path so black that she followed it by smell and by feel, rather than by sight. The dark made the way seem steeper, with far more turns and twists than in daylight. She brushed against dew-dampened ferns whose touch, once gentle, now seemed ominous and threatening.

Exhaustion took away some of her anger, and she began to think whether Thakur had been right after all. She also began to wonder if she should have left him without anyone else to help guard the treelings.

She climbed the last part of the trail, with her paws slipping on gravel made slick by spray and the booming of the fall in her ears. There was another sound, which grew louder as she approached the cave: the harsh roar of the Red Tongue.

Shadowy orange light spilling from the cave backlit the forms of the two Firekeepers who stood guard before the entrance. They rose, growling, but their challenge died to a mutter as they caught her smell.

"You have come to crouch before the Red Tongue, clan leader?"

"No. I have come to see Fessran."

The speaker glanced at his companion, who looked doubtfully back. "Before you enter, clan leader, there are some things you must not do . . ." He faltered under Ratha's glare and his ears twitched back.

"You dare tell me what I may do before the creature that I brought to the clan? *Ptaah!*" She lunged at them, striking out with teeth and claws.

Before either of the guards could recover, she was past them and into the gallery leading to the cave. She could tell at once that the fire was much larger than it had been. She could see her shadow on the rock floor of the gallery. A steady wind from outside blew past her, drawn to feed the hunger of the fire-creature.

Despite her anger, she hesitated. The light ahead dazzled her, and the heat swept over her in parching waves. For a moment, the fire seemed to hold her back; then her anger flared, forcing the fear aside.

She was in the cave itself. The Red Tongue's harsh and constant song filled the cavern and echoed back from the other chambers. The great fire reared up as if it was the central pillar that supported the cave, a writhing column of yellow and gold seeming to reach from floor to vaulted ceiling.

It lit the stone fangs that hung from the ceiling, turning them to a gleaming yellow that made them look even more like teeth in the mouth of a great and terrible creature.

Ratha was so awed by the Red Tongue itself that she almost didn't see the shapes that gathered around it. Their shadows stretched out toward her, wavering and dancing over the rubble-strewn floor until they passed over her. At first she thought the figures were Firekeepers stoking the great flame, but as she crept closer and her eyes grew accustomed to the fierce light, she saw that they were moving together in a circle around the fire. Their movements were slow and rhythmic, as if they were beginning a dance.

The longer Ratha watched, the more she was convinced that this was a dance, but one such as she had never seen. She remembered the dance-hunts she had used to celebrate the victory of the clan over the Un-Named. Those had been fierce and wild, but even the intensity of the dance-hunt didn't have the frenzy and fierceness of this.

The dancers leaped, lashed their flanks with their tails and struck out with their claws as if against some unseen but hated enemy. They reared up on their hind paws and reached toward the ceiling, twisting and writhing in the heat as if they themselves were the branches that were being consumed by the fire-creature in its endless hunger.

They shrieked aloud, and whether it was joy or terror in those cries, Ratha did not know. Their faces bore a look that none of the Named had ever held before, a look that was nearly madness. It was the wish to join themselves with the power of something far greater than themselves, even if it meant the sacrifice of their own wills.

The pounding rush and roar formed a rhythm for the dance, and even Ratha felt the strange tug of wild ecstasy that filled the eyes and bodies of the dancers. Amid the leaping figures, Ratha saw Fessran herself, her mouth stretched open in a cry of celebration to the power of the Red Tongue. She bounded higher than Ratha had ever seen her leap before, twisted herself in impossible ways and came so near the fire that Ratha trembled for fear she would fall in.

Ratha was so absorbed by the fire-dance that she didn't hear someone creep up behind her until his voice was in her ear.

"Yesss," he hissed. "Watch. Watch how it draws them, how it makes them dance. Look how it inspires them, clan leader, in a way that you cannot."

Ratha flinched away from Shongshar, but she was too dazed by the scene to do more than take a swipe at him. When her attention swung back to the dancers, he sidled up to her and began to speak again, his words blending in some strange way into the cries of the dancers and the harsh song of the fire. Hypnotized, she listened, unable to break the trance that had fallen across her.

"What is the skill of treelings compared to this?" Shongshar whispered. "Ah, clan leader, you never understood the real power of the creature you tamed. You left that understanding to me."

Ratha shuddered, but she could not take her eyes from the frenzied circle around the Red Tongue, nor could she block his voice from her ears.

"See what it does to your people. See how it pushes them beyond themselves. See how it takes them and fills them with strength and joy so that they have to leap and cry out. Join them, clan leader. Join them in their dance to the Red Tongue."

Angrily, Ratha spat at him and her slash drew blood, but he didn't strike back. She could see in his eyes that he knew she trembled. Her smell betrayed everything: rage, helplessness, fear, disgust and horrified fascination. She could see in his half-closed eyes that he knew she was close to the edge and that he would only have to wait for her to fall.

"Your mistake, clan leader," he said softly, "is in thinking that the fire-creature is just something to be used to protect us against the Un-Named Ones and to warm us by night. It is that, but it is something much more."

"It is the egg of a fly that turns a carcass rotten. It is the wound that starts an abscess under the skin," she hissed, desperately seeking the strength of her anger and trying not to see how high the Firekeepers leaped in the terrifying beauty of the dance.

"If that is how you choose to think of it, clan leader," Shongshar said placidly.

"Why aren't you part of the dance?" Ratha demanded, but even as she spoke, she knew the answer. One who understood the Red Tongue's power as well as he did would not be easily controlled by it.

"I am part of it in my own way," he said and as he spoke the firelight flashed on his sabers, reminding her that he did not need any power other than his own to be dangerous. He eyed her and grinned at her discomfort. "Perhaps you shouldn't wait for the dance to finish, clan leader. You've left Thakur alone with the treeling creatures. Since you seem to value them for reasons I don't quite understand, you wouldn't want anything to happen to them, would you?"

Ratha stiffened, her rage paralyzing her tongue. "You wouldn't dare!" she finally spat.

"Me? Certainly not. But there are others who dislike the idea of the clan leader dirtying herself with those animals."

"And you wouldn't raise a paw to stop anyone from doing such a thing. Let me tell you this, Shongshar. If any one of the Firekeepers even makes a threat against Thakur or his treelings, this cave will be closed down and the Red Tongue will die. Do you understand me?"

"Yes, I do," he said in a silky voice that was almost a purr. "But to be sure, I would also ask them." He flicked his whiskers at the dancers. His voice hardened. "And then I would ask them who they obey. It might surprise you, clan leader."

His eyes still held their same orange glint, but now a cold ruthlessness came into them. Their hate struck into Ratha as if he had slashed her with his fangs, and she backed away from him, trembling with fear and the cold certainty that she had left Thakur and the treelings open to attack.

She whirled and sprinted away from him, across the shadows that still danced and flickered on the cave floor, through the gallery and out into the darkness. The fire-creature's fading roar became a mocking howl as she slipped and skidded on the graveled trail and fought to find her way with eyes that had been made night-blind by the angry light.

Thakur, you told me not to go and again you were right. I was too angry to listen, but anger does me no good now. There was a bright spot before her eyes where she had looked at the heart of the cave-fire, and she could only see in front of her by turning her head from side to side as she ran. By the time she reached the path to Thakur's den, her sight had recovered, but she could not find the welcoming flicker of the little fire she had left with him.

She thought at first that her panic might have led her down the wrong trail, but the scents about her and the feel of the ground were right. She peered ahead, her growing apprehension choking her throat and tightening her chest. The smell of smoldering ashes drew her to the remains of the fire she had left. It had been broken and scattered.

The ashy acrid smell was strong, and mixed in with it were traces of other scents that she could detect but not recognize. There were pugmarks faintly visible in the starlight, but they were smeared, as if whoever made them had slipped while running.

"Thakur . . . ," she moaned softly, her whiskers trembling. "Aree . . . Ratharee . . ." She approached a shape on the ground and touched it tentatively with her paw, fearing it might be the torn body of a treeling. It was only a broken branch from the scattered fire, and she sighed with relief as it rolled under her paw.

She made her way to the den itself and crawled inside, thinking a treeling might have taken shelter there, but the den was cold and empty except for the same ashy smell that filled the air outside.

When Ratha left the den she froze at the sight of two amber eyes staring at her from the night-shadow of a tree. The eyes blinked and moved forward. Ratha arched her back and flared her tail, unable to catch the newcomer's scent in the wind that blew away from her.

"Clan leader?" The voice was female and quavery with uncertainty.

"Who is that?" Ratha snarled. "Are you a Firekeeper?"

"I'm Bira. Clan leader, come with me. I know where Thakur is."

Her first impulse was to follow Bira eagerly, but caution held her back. Young and friendly as Bira was, she belonged with those who tended the Red Tongue.

"How do I know that Shongshar hasn't sent you?"

"He sent me down with those who were to kill the treelings, but I turned on them and fought beside Thakur," Bira answered. "If you want proof, here is the ash that I rubbed into my pelt to disguise myself like them, and here is the bite on my foreleg from Nyang's teeth."

Bira came forward, letting Ratha smell her fur. As she approached, Ratha saw a small shape crouched on Bira's neck. "Thakur told me to bring your treeling, and she came with me, even though she was still frightened," said the young Firekeeper. "Here." She came alongside and Ratha felt treeling paws grasp her fur as Ratharee climbed from Bira's back to hers. The treeling wound its tail around her neck and hugged her fiercely, its trembling telling her how lost and frightened it had been.

Ratha suddenly felt steadier. Bira wouldn't have brought Ratharee in order to lead her into a trap. If Shongshar wanted to have her killed, there were other, easier ways. The young female's story sounded true and there was no taint of deceit in either her words or her smell.

"Hurry, clan leader! Once Shongshar knows I have betrayed him, he will send others after me."

"All right, Bira. Take me to Thakur."

She followed Bira down the path until it met the main trail. As soon as Bira took the turn that led to the creek trail, Ratha's suspicion flared again, and she followed warily, testing the air for scents of hidden attackers. Soon, however, Bira cut off the creek trail and began to climb the steep bank above it. Before long they were in the deeper darkness amid the great trees, and Ratha's paws fell on crumbled bark and pine needles.

Ratha sensed they were making a wide circle to avoid the base of the falls and the cave that sheltered the Red Tongue. She wondered if Fessran and the others were still at their wild dance. The thought made her shiver.

"We're going to some little caves above the falls. I found them one day when I was exploring, and no one else knows about them," Bira explained as Ratha padded beside her. "I brought Thakur up this far, told him where to find the place and then went back down to look for you."

"Did you save all the treelings?"

"Yes. One of the little ones got a scratch and Aree's a bit bruised, but they're all right."

Some of the tension seeped out of Ratha and she concentrated on climbing. At last they found an old trail that had many rises and drops as well as endless switchbacks. Ratha was sure they must be far beyond clan ground when Bira turned off the path and disappeared down a brush-covered slope. The way led into a little vale with the sound of a brook chuckling over rocks and the glint of starlight on foaming water. Bira ran along the near bank and ducked under a great gray slab of broken rock.

Now Ratha could throw her fear aside, for Thakur's scent was strong in the air about the streambank. Beneath the overhang were small recesses that barely qualified as caves. She found Thakur and the treelings nestled together in the largest one.

"Shh, Aree. It's only Ratha," he soothed as the largest of the treeling shapes lifted its muzzle in alarm. He shifted over to make room for Ratha on the soft sandy floor. Her relief at seeing him safe overwhelmed her, and for a while she could only crouch beside him, licking his ears, and saying, "Thakur, I should have listened. I should have listened," over and over.

"Well, I was lucky," he said when she finally calmed down. "The Firekeepers weren't really after me, just the treelings. And when Bira turned and started helping me fight, that really confused them. That gave us time to gather up the treelings and run."

"We nearly lost Aree," added the young Firekeeper. "When Nyang scratched one of her cubs, she flew at him and bit him hard. You should have heard him yell."

"Nyang again," Ratha said with distaste. "He will do anything for Shongshar, won't he? I imagine he was the one who pushed Bundi into the fire."

"He led us," said Bira. "He showed us how to rub ashes into our pelts so that no one could smell who we were. I hate the taste and feel of it; I'm going to wash myself in the stream tomorrow."

"Bira," Ratha said slowly, "I'm grateful to you for what you did. You had no reason to want to help me. You wouldn't have had a witless litter if I hadn't let Shongshar into the clan."

"You took your chance, clan leader, and I took mine," Bira answered. "I grieved for that litter, but now they are gone I don't think of them any more. As for Thakur, I was the one who built the fire for him when he was teaching

Aree. I liked him and I liked the treelings too much to let Shongshar kill them, so I tried to make Nyang think I was fierce and nasty enough for his group of killers. It wasn't easy," she added with a grimace that narrowed the glow of her eyes.

"I think," said Thakur firmly, "that we should get some sleep. Whatever is happening has just begun, and we are going to need all our strength and cleverness tomorrow."

Although his words sounded somber, Ratha was too tired to worry. Bira offered to stand guard through the first part of the night and Thakur said he would take the following watch. He hadn't finished speaking when his voice became a drone that faded in Ratha's ears as she slid into sleep.

She woke suddenly, shaking away the dream-image of a huge fire with grotesque black figures leaping through the flames. She opened her eyes and gratefully breathed the air of a quiet morning. Somewhere a bird trilled a high sweet note over the merry noise of the stream. Bira slept alongside, her head on her paws, her flanks rising and falling slowly. Ratharee was curled between them, the treeling's brown-black fur contrasting with Bira's ash-streaked red and Ratha's own fawn color.

She lifted her muzzle and focused on Thakur, who was sitting just outside the little cave. Ratha yawned and then crept out, trying not to disturb either Bira or the treelings. She stretched, gathering herself together for the new day.

"No one knows what happened last night except Shongshar, Nyang's group of Firekeepers and ourselves," she said thoughtfully. "None of them are going to tell anyone, especially since their attempt was a failure, thanks to Bira."

"What are you going to do?" asked Thakur. "Talk to Fessran?"

Ratha fell silent. After seeing the Firekeeper leader in her frenzied dance before the Red Tongue, she doubted that Fessran would listen to anything about treelings or even about Shongshar's misdeeds.

"No," she said. "I'm going to talk to the herders and tell them what Shongshar is up to. Then I'm going to lead them up the creek trail and take all the wood out of the cave. Without wood, the cave-fire will die and so will Shongshar's power. We'll see who obeys him then!"

"It may not be so easy." The herding teacher looked at her, his eyes full of doubt.

"It won't be, but if I can hold the loyalty of the herders, I can do it. Come with me, Thakur. Cherfan and the other herders will be more likely to listen to me if you are there."

"And I am less likely to get pounced upon by Nyang and his pack of Firekeepers," said Thakur dryly and added, "I didn't think I would do much teaching today."

"Can we trust Bira to stay with the treelings?"

"Yes. She's no longer a Firekeeper. They wouldn't take her back after she turned on them to help me. Nyang's probably looking for her, and she knows she's safe here."

Ratha stared into the cave, taking one last look at Ratharee. "I hope Bira can keep the treelings safe." She turned to face Thakur and felt a shiver at the solemn look on his face.

"You aren't sure about this either, are you."

"No," he admitted.

There was nothing else to be said. She led the way out

from under the overhang, and they waded in the stream for a distance so that their scents and prints wouldn't lead anyone to Bira. Then they cut back to the trail and set off downhill for the meadow.

CHAPTER 16

RATHA AND THAKUR didn't meet anyone on the trails they took. Even the path to the meadow was deserted and, when Ratha reached the trailhead and gazed out across the grass, she sensed a tense stillness in the morning air.

She saw the dapplebacks and three-horns gathered in a tight flock instead of being scattered across the pasture as they usually were in the morning. Around the edge of the meadow, several guard-fires still burned. That was strange, she thought. Usually the Firekeepers put them out after sunrise.

The herdbeasts didn't like being confined to such a small area of meadow. Ratha could hear the three-horns bray and paw the ground, while the dapplebacks snorted and whinnied. A few herders circled the animals, trotting around the flock to keep it together. The others were nowhere in sight.

"Ratha!" A deep voice drew her attention away from the animals. Cherfan bounded toward her over the grass. She could tell from the urgency in the big herder's stride and the way his whiskers trembled that he was worried.

"Where is everyone, Cherfan?" Thakur asked calmly.

"Behind the big thorn thicket near the far end of the meadow. Someone killed a dappleback early this morning," he said, turning to Ratha.

"Un-Named raiders? Bristlemanes?"

"I don't think so. Nothing broke through the line of guard-fires."

Ratha began pacing beside him with Thakur at her flank. "Have you found the carcass?"

"No, but we found the place where the animal was brought down." Cherfan broke into a fast lope and Ratha galloped beside him until they reached the thornbush. Behind it was a hidden stretch of meadow and she could tell by the torn and flattened grass that the herdbeast had died here.

Gathered around the spot were the rest of the herders, sniffing the ground and exchanging puzzled looks. Cherfan stepped into their midst, waving his tail. He stopped and looked them over carefully. "That's strange," he growled. "We're missing someone. Where's Shoman?"

The herders muttered among themselves and soon confirmed that Shoman was not helping to guard the remaining animals, nor was he anywhere else in the meadow. In fact, no one remembered having seen him since the middle of the night.

"And Bundi's not here either," said Thakur abruptly.

"There's something else I don't understand." Cherfan narrowed his eyes. "We keep the dapplebacks out in the center of the meadow during the night. We don't let them go behind these bushes; it's too easy for them to wander away. If someone killed a mare here, he would have had to drive it away from the flock and the beast would have fought and made enough noise to bring all of us running."

"Unless it was lured here by someone it knew," said Ratha.

"All right. The dappleback may have been lured here and then killed, but none of us heard it scream. A dappleback will cry out when it feels the touch of fangs."

"Not if there are a pair of attackers," Thakur said quickly. "One lures the beast while the other hides. When the beast is distracted, the other leaps out and bites behind the head. The creature dies quickly and quietly. I've used the same method in culling."

Cherfan wrinkled the fur on his brow. "Shoman . . . and Bundi? Perhaps Shoman would do such a thing. I've never trusted him. But Bundi?"

"I caught Shoman with a piece of meat he was using to bribe a Firekeeper," Ratha reminded him. "Bundi was with him. He said they were both being shunned by the rest of you because of their injuries from the Red Tongue."

"Shoman killed that dappleback to revenge himself on us?" Cherfan's puzzlement began to give way to anger.

"Not for revenge," said Ratha. "I think he was forced to lure it here and kill it."

"Forced? By whom? And where is the meat? He and Bundi couldn't have eaten it by themselves."

Ratha glanced at Thakur, then turned her gaze back to Cherfan. "You will find the carcass in the cave where the Red Tongue is kept."

A wave of mutters and growls spread through the herders. Some looked uncertain while others raised the fur on their napes and showed their fangs. Cherfan flattened his ears. "You're saying that Shoman killed the beast for Shongshar and Fessran? Why?"

"Because he and Bundi were made outcasts by the Red

Tongue's mark and sought to placate the Firekeepers by any way possible. Shongshar knew his desperation and used him," Ratha hissed.

A wave of muttering and growling spread among the herders. Cherfan flattened his ears. "No one is allowed to kill herdbeasts without your order."

"And I did not order anyone to take that animal," said Ratha, staring meaningfully at the other herders. "Shongshar and Fessran have disobeyed me and clan law. The carcass is stolen meat and they have no right to it. If the Firekeepers are left unpunished, they will steal again and the rest of us will go hungry." She paused and then growled, "Do you want to hear your bellies rumble because of the Firekeepers' greed?"

"No!" came the answer in many voices. "Lead us to the cave and we will take back the stolen meat."

"Listen to me," cried Ratha. "It is the Red Tongue in the cave that gives the Firekeepers their strength. They have stored wood there to feed it. If we take back the wood as well as the meat, the cave-fire will starve and die."

"We will take back what they have stolen!"

"You do not fear the Firekeepers?"

A chorus of roars and howls rose from the group. "There are more of us than there are of them. To the cave!"

With Thakur and Cherfan flanking her, Ratha led the outraged herders up the creek trail. At first the group was boisterous and noisy, but as they drew close enough to hear the song of the Red Tongue, they became quiet. Uncertain looks passed back and forth among the herders and Ratha knew that the sense of awe that subdued those who came before the fire-creature was creeping over them again.

Thakur could sense it too, for he put his muzzle to her ear and whispered, "Don't hesitate, Ratha, or these brave herders will desert us."

She was grateful for the smell of dappleback meat that lingered in the air along the path. The scent fanned the herders' anger anew and kept them pacing steadily behind her. When they reached the last stretch of the trail, Ratha whispered her final instructions.

With a roar as loud as the booming of the falls, her pack charged the cave entrance and the two Firekeeper guards. The guards tried to fight, but only managed to avoid being trampled as the herders knocked them aside and surged into the cave.

Again the fire-creature rose up before her, writhing and hissing like a live thing, but this time, Ratha was too angry to be cowed by the sight. She looked beyond the fire to where a group of Firekeepers pulled and tore at a half-stripped carcass. Nyang lifted his head, his muzzle ash-streaked and bloody. Fessran dropped the haunch she was chewing and stood up while the others glared back at Ratha over the bared ribs of the kill.

Only Shongshar continued to eat, holding a chunk of liver between his paws and slicing it with his side teeth. Ratha could hear muffled growls among the herders, but none of them came forward to challenge the Firekeepers at their feast. Many of them glanced uneasily at the Red Tongue in the center of the cave, as if expecting it to leap out and sear the first herder who made a move.

Ratha turned her gaze to Fessran. Fessran stared back haughtily, but a flicker of guilt crossed her face. "This meat is forbidden," Ratha said in a voice that echoed around the walls of the cavern. "Leave it."

Some of the Firekeepers exchanged glances and a few backed away from the kill.

"No!" Fessran leaped over the carcass and stood before it, lashing her tail. "We who serve the Red Tongue have taken what is rightfully ours. Eat without shame, Fire-keepers, for it is the creature that we tend that guards the herd from raiders."

"Yes, Fessran. Tell them to eat without shame from a beast killed wrongly and dragged to a cave in secret," Ratha snarled.

"When those who keep the herdbeasts hold back meat from us who watch the guard-fires, then we have a right to such a kill," cried Nyang, from behind Fessran.

"*Ptahh!* All in the clan have an equal chance to fill their bellies when the kill is eaten where it falls. Anything else is greed or arrogance, litterling." Ratha glared at Nyang, but he ducked behind Fessran.

"What you think is equal, clan leader, is not enough for us," Fessran said. "Serving the Red Tongue is difficult work, and it is a long way to the meadow."

Ratha spat again. "You shame yourself by speaking lies you don't even believe, Firekeeper leader. You know as well as I that to steal and hoard meat from a kill is an act that strikes out against the clan and my leadership." She met their stares one by one until she fixed her eyes on Fessran. "Who ordered that herdbeast to be taken without my knowledge. Was it you, Fessran?"

"The beast was killed by herders." The Firekeeper leader spoke sullenly.

"Yes, by a pair of herders who were told that they had to lure the beast and slaughter it in return for being allowed to enter this cave. In return for being allowed to crouch before the creature that I brought to serve the Named, but which now has birthed a litter that feeds from us like cubs from their mother."

"You dare!" Fessran's eyes were blazing. "You dare to speak of us that way. We serve the power of the Red Tongue, clan leader, and that power answers to none except itself!"

Ratha waited until the echoes of Fessran's voice had faded into the hollow roar of the cave-fire. "Are those words your own, Firekeeper?" she asked with bitter sorrow thick in her throat. "Did you force Shoman and Bundi to make that kill?"

Fessran tried to answer, but the word would not leave her tongue. She stood, shaking, staring down at the floor between her feet.

"I did. I did!" screamed Nyang, lunging over the kill to face Ratha. His face, stained with blood and distorted by hate, was no longer that of an older cub but of someone filled with menace and malevolence.

"No, you wretched cub!" Fessran seized his scruff as he crouched to spring at Ratha and wrenched him off his feet. She threw him aside with a powerful toss of her head and flattened her ears at him. He crawled away, his eyes smoldering.

Ratha's stare was suddenly drawn to Shongshar, who had finished the dappleback's liver and now sat up. He began to clean his paws, but he interrupted this task to lift his head and fix his gaze on Ratha.

She felt as though she could fall into those eyes and be consumed by the flame that burned behind them, without leaving so much as a charred bone. The orange in them shimmered and writhed as if she saw into them through waves of terrible heat. Now she knew where the true power of the Red Tongue lay. Not in the fire burning within the cave, but in the depths of those eyes.

She knew that she had helped to lay the kindling for this fire of the spirit that had taken grief into its fierce heart and blackened it into hate. The herders saw it too and many turned their faces away from him.

"Shongshar," she said softly, yet her voice seemed to ring about her in the cavern.

"The order to kill the dappleback was mine, clan leader," he answered and continued to lick his paw.

"Why?"

"So that the Firekeepers might feast. The herding teacher beside you knows that cubs learn well if they have had enough to eat, and they are more willing to listen to the one who has fed them."

Ratha waited. Shongshar paced forward and took Fessran's place without even looking at her. She melted away from him with a frightened glance that left no doubt who was the real leader of the Firekeepers.

Shongshar spoke again. "The beast was not killed just for food, clan leader. There is another kind of hunger in your people, and it is one that a full belly will not satisfy. You do not understand this hunger, and you have done nothing to feed it. But it is a hunger that I know well."

Ratha shivered, held against her will by the spell of his voice and the depths of his eyes.

"Look around you, and you will see it in the eyes of your herders as well as the Firekeepers," said Shongshar, with a strange compelling rhythm in his speech. "Look within you and you will see it there."

Despite herself, Ratha found her gaze traveling over the faces of the herders. They were silent, held as she was by the sibilant sound of Shongshar's voice. And yes, he was right. In their faces, in their eyes and even in the changing scents of their smells, she felt a longing that perhaps had always been there, or perhaps had just been conjured out of them by the power of his words. She didn't know which it was, and that knowledge made her afraid.

Within herself she sensed the same hunger, a feeling that she had never been able to put words to. It was a strange hunger that crept up inside her when she was alone looking up at the stars. It had come upon her when she had first sought a mate; in the closeness with him, it had nearly been filled. And it was the same hunger that drew her to the dance she had seen around the Red Tongue even as she had feared it.

And she knew that the search to satisfy this strange need could lead to things that were good, such as seeing the fluffy beauty of a newborn cub or the sheen of a dappleback stallion's coat as he pranced about the meadow. Yet the same hunger could be twisted into something that could flourish in the depths of a cave, feeding on hatred amidst bones and tainted flesh.

Shongshar knew how to feed it; she had no doubt of that. It was as if he had fathered a litter that suckled not milk, but blood. Her horror and her anger gave her the strength to tear her gaze away from his and turn his words aside.

"Herders! Listen to me!" she cried. "The need he speaks of is really his own. If you give yourselves and your beasts to the will of the creature he serves, you will be the meat that feeds him."

"No!" the herders cried, but many voices were missing, and those she heard sounded thin and ragged with doubt.

It was too late to command them to attack the Firekeepers. She didn't know how many of the herders who had spoken so bravely down in the meadow would stand by her if it came to an open battle. Even as they stood beside her, she sensed their courage being stolen from them by the raging creature in the center of the cave from which Shongshar drew his power. It was there that she would have to strike.

"The wood," whispered Thakur softly behind her. "They have forgotten about it."

She glanced at the side of the cave, to where stacks of branches and kindling lay. Then she looked at the herders and hoped they would follow her. With Thakur at her flank, she leaped up and galloped toward the woodpile.

For an instant she thought she and Thakur would have to face the Firekeepers alone. Then Cherfan plunged after her and the herders followed. They reached the woodpile before the other side could rally and cut them off. Ratha saw that the Firekeepers had mistaken the herders' charge for an attack on the carcass and had massed together to defend their kill.

"Form a line so none of them can get through," Ratha said and her pack spread themselves out, guarding the woodpile. Nyang and several other Firekeepers approached, but they soon retreated from the menacing growls and bared fangs of the defenders.

She paced across in front of her own line and faced Shongshar. He looked at her and said nothing as she sat and curled her tail across her feet.

"You may eat, Firekeepers," she said, turning her gaze toward them, "but this will be your last meal in this cave by the Red Tongue's light."

Her words were met with snarls and jeers. Soon, however, the Firekeepers grew tired of taunting her pack and turned their attention to the kill, dragging it around on the cave floor as they wrenched chunks of flesh loose and gulped them down. They did not seem to notice that the fire had already begun to fall and that their shadows were growing longer. Only Shongshar did not eat with them. He sat and watched the herders through slitted eyes.

When the carcass was stripped, the Firekeepers again amused themselves by throwing insults at the herders and trying to break through their line, but Ratha could see that the effort was half-hearted. The grim response the herders gave them quickly discouraged any idea that this was fun.

Shongshar continued to watch, and Ratha sensed that he was waiting. For what, she didn't know, and she grew uneasy. His strength was waning with the falling fire, yet he made no attempt to launch an attack. He only sat and studied the herders' faces with an acuteness that made them show their fangs and then try to look away from him.

The Firekeepers groomed themselves, or lay and slept as if the herders weren't there. Shadows crept in from the sides of the cave and the dying fire's light turned ruddy. The fire began to smoke and flicker. The flame no longer drew the wind from outside, and the cave started to fill with smoky haze.

Ratha was stiff from sitting and was about to get up and move to ease her legs when she heard Shongshar's voice. It had grown so dim in the cave that she could see only his eyes, which now burned brighter than the fire.

"Let it die, then, clan leader," he hissed. "Let it die and give this den back to darkness. It is better that we have nothing to crouch down before or nothing to dance to in wild joy. It is better that we of the Named turn our backs on something as great as this, for we are too weak to hold it within our jaws."

Ratha heard whispered mutters behind her and the looks she received were shadowed by doubt. Even Cherfan seemed lost and gazed at Shongshar as if he might find a refuge in his words.

She had no answer for Shongshar except stern silence, and soon his voice came again.

"Watch this creature die, you of the clan, and see the death of all you could be. The Named could rule far beyond clan ground and be so fierce and terrible that all who once preyed on us would either flee or throw themselves at our feet. That is the power you are throwing away if you obey her."

Again voices buzzed behind her, and eyes grew bright with visions of such a future.

"Be silent!" she hissed, as much at them as at Shongshar. The flame sank into its bed of ashes and tumbled coals. Slowly the fierce red glow faded.

Ratha felt herself start to tremble with the triumph of her victory. The cave-fire was dead and Shongshar's power crippled. She waited, feeling the air around her grow cool.

"It is over," she said, rising. "Firekeepers, leave the cave."

One by one, they passed in front of her, with lowered heads and dragging tails until only one was left. Shongshar.

"Do you come, or do I have you dragged out?" she growled.

The two orange slits glared at her from the blackness.

His form was a deeper darkness than that of the cave and she tensed, fearing that he would use the instant that he passed her to strike out at her.

Suddenly the eyes were gone. She saw them again as she heard coals break under the slap of his paw.

"You of the clan!" he roared. "Look! It lives!"

A tiny flame burst from the broken embers and grew as he breathed on it. Then she heard the sound of running feet, and before she could fling herself toward the fire to scatter it and beat out the remaining life, she saw that someone had broken from the herders' ranks, bringing Shongshar wood and tinder.

Her roar of rage filled the cave and she charged him, but several more herders had already joined him and they threw her back. She struck hard, rolled over, and when she staggered to her feet again, the flame was rekindled, surging up with new strength.

Shongshar's roar called the Firekeepers back into the cave. They mingled with the deserting herders until Ratha could no longer tell them apart. Even those herders that tried to stay with her were seized and dragged away from their positions by the woodpile. She saw Cherfan's despairing look as he was surrounded by Firekeepers and forced to the back of the cave.

The fire crackled with malicious energy as it consumed the new offerings of wood that were laid upon it. Ratha saw by the harsh light that only Thakur stood beside her, his nape and tail flared, his lips drawn back from his fangs.

"Take the herding teacher," Shongshar commanded, standing near the flames. "He is the one who would mock us by giving the keeping of the Red Tongue to treelings. Bring him here and have him bare his throat."

Nyang led the eager pack that fell on Thakur. Ratha leaped on them, raking their backs and their ears, but again she was flung aside and could only look on as Thakur fought with savage desperation. He bloodied several pelts before they subdued him. Teeth fastened on his scruff, his forelegs, his tail; someone got their jaws around his muzzle to keep him from biting.

Slowly they dragged him, writhing and kicking, toward the fire. His claws, dragging on the rock, made a sound like the death shriek of a herdbeast. There was a gasp that made Ratha glance toward Fessran and she saw the Firekeeper's eyes grow wide with horror and helplessness.

Once more she flung herself at Thakur's captors, but another pack pulled her off and held her. They brought her close and forced her to watch.

"Now, herding teacher," said Shongshar, leering at Thakur. "Bare your throat to the Red Tongue."

Again Thakur fought, but again he was stilled. His captors pulled him closer to the flames and forced his head back so his throat lay open and exposed.

"I bare it, but it is to you I bare it, Shongshar," he growled between his teeth. "This talk of serving the Red Tongue's power is nothing but a lie."

They shook him to silence him. Ratha thought then that Shongshar would slash Thakur's throat with his long fangs, but he stepped back from the herding teacher with satisfaction on his face.

"Good. He has begun to show his loyalty. Hold him. We will need him to guide us to the renegade Firekeeper Bira and the treelings."

He turned, fixing his eyes on Ratha, filling her with an icy fear that she could not overcome with anger. He began to pace toward her, seeming to grow with each step.

The Firekeepers that held Ratha drew back, leaving her alone facing him.

"You are worthy of my fangs, clan leader," he said softly. "You know I can't leave you alive. If you lie still, I will be quick."

Ratha dodged his first strike. They circled each other, ears flat, tails lashing. She forced her trembling legs to tighten for a spring and she leaped onto his back, driving her teeth into the side of his neck. He shuddered, but did not fall, even as she threw her weight out to drag him off balance. His blood welled into her mouth, but she knew her strike was not a killing wound.

He shook her to the side and rolled on her, but she kept her jaws locked, despite his crushing weight. Her teeth sank deeper, and she flung her forelegs around his neck, adding their pull to the strength of her straining jaws. He wrenched his head back and forth, but he could not break free, and she thought for an instant that she might be able to keep her hold until loss of blood weakened him.

He shoved a paw between her chest and his and began to pry her away. She could not sustain her grip against his powerful forelegs. She twisted her head, trying to bite deeper, but her teeth tore from the wound. The great pressure of his massive paw against her chest threatened to crush her ribs, and she drew short painful breaths.

She lost her hold and he forced her to the cave floor, one paw on her neck, the other on her chest. She writhed and wriggled, but only exhausted herself.

Above her, his teeth gleamed and his eyes burned. His jaw dropped far down, exposing the full and terrible length of his fangs. He lowered his head, and she felt the hard curve against the pulsing of her throat. His claws drove into her to hold her still as he reared his head back for the killing downslash.

"Ratha!" The scream filled the cave. From the corner of her eye, she saw the circle of herders give way as someone burst through. She grunted at the sudden impact of a body hurtling on top of her own and felt scrabbling claws as Fessran's smell washed over her.

Ratha caught a glimpse of Shongshar's fangs driving down toward her; then Fessran heaved and jerked. She felt the shock as Shongshar struck and heard the shriek of teeth against bone. She wrenched herself out from beneath them as a dismayed hiss welled up from those watching.

In her blurred sight, Shongshar lifted his reddened fangs from the body of the Firekeeper who had once been her friend.

"I bare my throat to you again, Ratha," Fessran whispered, rolling her head to look up at her. "Forgive my foolishness."

A sudden commotion broke out near the fire. One of the Firekeepers guarding Thakur recoiled from his slash. Using the moment of confusion to break free, he streaked across the cave floor to Ratha.

"Run!" he cried. She gave Fessran one last, despairing look and plunged after Thakur as he passed her. They dashed out of the cavern, down the gallery, and were out in the sunlight before roars and howls broke from the cave behind them.

Thakur rushed to the stream that spilled from the base of the falls, leaping from rock to rock until he was nearly lost in the spray. She followed, fighting to keep her footing on slick stones. He ran downstream and leaped onto the bole of a tree that leaned out from the steep slope rising before them. She sprang up behind him and together they bounded through the brush until they reached the crest of the hill.

"That should confuse them," Thakur panted, looking back. "They'll think we took the trail."

Ratha was too numb to hear his words. She still seemed to feel the shock and shudder as Fessran took the strike meant for her. Softly she moaned her friend's name aloud.

"Ratha," Thakur said. "Ratha, there's no hope for her. Even if he hasn't killed her, she will die soon. Those fangs went deep."

"I should go back and take my revenge on him. I should fight for my place as clan leader," she hissed, rage and despair choking her throat.

"And there will be another of the Named to lie bleeding on the floor in the Red Tongue's den. Without you, neither Bira nor I have any hope. The time is past when you can listen to anger," he said, and Ratha knew he was right.

The sound of angry calls below sent them running up the slope of the next hill.

"Soon the Firekeepers will find our track," said Thakur. "We should split up and draw them away from where Bira and the treelings are hiding."

"I'll draw them. You circle back, find Bira and tell her what has happened. Don't worry," she said, at his doubtful look. "I won't try to turn and fight them. I'll meet you at the little cave by the stream."

"All right." He flicked his tail and trotted uphill. After he was gone, she went back along his path, smearing out his pugmarks and covering his smell with hers. Satisfied that she had concealed his trail, she glanced at the sun and galloped down the slope, away from the cries that told her that Shongshar and the Firekeepers had found her tracks.

CHAPTER 17

RESTING BRIEFLY, Ratha leaned on a dew-dampened rock, laying her cheek against its coolness. She heard the Firekeepers crashing through brush and dead leaves. She could see the approaching flicker of their firebrands through the trees and sensed that once again they were picking up her trail. A shiver that was half fear and half excitement ran through her.

She was glad, however, that the Firekeepers had chosen to track her by torchlight. A scent trail, which they might have followed easily in the damp night air, became difficult and elusive in the smoky haze from the torches. No. Shongshar knew better than to think he would catch her this way. He had brought out the torchbearers to show the Red Tongue's wrath and let her own fear drive her like a renegade from clan ground.

She grinned bitterly as she ran across a patch of hair-ferns that made no rustle to give her away. She had already seen the worst that the fire-creature could do. It could burn flesh and bone and even forest, but it could also possess the minds and twist the wills of her people as if they were pieces of bark glowing and curling in the heart of the flame.

The sky above the treetops showed deep violet and the glittering stars were dimming. Ratha realized, looking up, that she had been leading the Firekeepers astray all night. Thakur would have had plenty of time to reach Bira. It was time to put an end to this cub's play before daylight gave the searchers additional advantage.

She crept away a little farther and listened. Again they had come to a halt and were casting about for signs of her. She spat quietly to herself, disgusted with the noise they were making, and then slipped away through the underbrush.

She kept to the edge of clan ground to avoid being seen by accident. To conceal her trail, she frequently backtracked, waded in streams and rolled in the dung of other animals to disguise her smell.

The sun was just showing over the treetops when she reached the sandy path that led beneath the overhang to the cave where she, Bira, Thakur and the treelings had spent the previous night. She had a bad moment when she discovered that particular hollow empty. She was nervously searching the other caves when the sound of Thakur's voice came from the shadows beneath the overhang.

"Over here," he said. "We've moved our hiding place.'

Her relief made her nearly collapse on the sand, but she only lolled her tongue out and padded after him.

Thakur led her farther upstream, to a smaller fall where the water cascaded down onto split stones that turned it into many tumbling rivulets. Ratha turned for a moment to watch the morning light dance and run down the falling water. Then she glimpsed Thakur's tail disappearing between two slabs of rock that leaned against each other.

She followed him, reluctant to leave the cheerful morning and go into the dimness of a cave. When she was inside, however, she found the tilted stone floor dappled with sunlight and shadow and felt a breeze that carried the fresh smell and sound of the little fall. It was sufficient shelter to keep anyone who hid within from being seen, yet it was open enough not to feel confining.

Bira lay in a sun-washed hollow with the treelings gathered around her and on top of her. Ratha looked for Ratharee and saw the young one's black eyes gleam as Ratharee spotted her. With a squeal of joy, the treeling scampered up the sloping rock and launched herself at her companion.

"Ooof. She's getting heavy, Thakur," Ratha groaned, but she couldn't quite make her voice sound convincingly plaintive. Once the treeling had taken her usual place on Ratha's shoulder with her tail curled around her neck, Ratha stretched out in a pool of sun near Thakur and Bira.

For a while, they lay there, quietly relaxed, and Ratha felt herself drifting into a light doze. Then Thakur sat up, with Aree perched on his shoulder, and said, "We must talk."

Ratha yawned and shook away her drowsiness. "Does Bira know what happened last night?"

"Yes, Thakur told me," Bira answered. "I'm not surprised that the herders deserted you. Shongshar seems able to persuade anyone to do anything."

"There were some things I should have said," Ratha growled, laying her head on her paws and feeling the helplessness and rage sweep over her again. "I should have told them that his talk about the Named ruling beyond clan ground was a mad cub's dream. I should have torn apart the herder who brought Shongshar the kindling. And I should have known that trying to kill the Red Tongue by starving it was exactly what Shongshar wanted me to do."

"Extending his rule may not be a mad cub's dream for him," said Thakur thoughtfully. "If he can make the Firekeepers fierce and arrogant, they can hold more territory and the herders can graze more animals. This may be difficult to face, but we have to admit that Shongshar has offered the Named a way not only to survive, but to flourish."

"*Ptahh!* They will be meat for his belly." Ratha spat. "They will grovel before the fire-creature in the cave and forget they once had wills of their own."

"Many of our people would rather follow the commands of a voice stronger than their own, even if it is cruel and harsh. We of the Named have a strange hate and an even stranger love for those who are powerful," Thakur said softly and added, "as you found when you first brought us this creature we call the Red Tongue."

Ratha sighed. "If I had known then what my creature would become to them, I never would have—" She caught herself. "No. Once it was done, there was no way I could go back."

"And we can't go back now. Shongshar holds the minds of our people just as surely as he holds the Red Tongue."

"He is only one and one can die," she snarled fiercely, making Ratharee start in alarm.

Thakur looked sadly back at her as she soothed her treeling. "That is not the answer, Ratha. Even if you succeeded in killing him, others would carry on his ideas. To regain your place as clan leader, you would have to destroy the cave and everything in it. I do not know how that could be done with only you, Bira and me."

"Are you going to give up and leave our people to become meat in Shongshar's jaws?" Angry indignation swept over her.

"Listen to me. Whatever prompted the choice of our people, they have made it. If you take Shongshar from them now, you will only earn your own death. Later, when his ways have made him hated, you may have a chance. You must wait and watch."

Bira shifted herself as a young treeling climbed down from her and went to its mother, who started to groom it. "I don't think we can stay here," she said. "We are still on clan ground and, although this place is hidden, Shongshar will eventually find it."

"I agree," said Thakur. "We must leave clan territory and live somewhere else for a while. There is a place I often go when I leave during the mating season. It isn't that far, and it has fruit trees, which will feed the treelings."

Reluctantly Ratha agreed with him. Her first thought had been to make this place their temporary home and use it to launch forays against the Firekeepers or try to undermine Shongshar's support among the herders. But she had to admit that Thakur was right. There wasn't much that their small group could do with the rest of the clan against them. It was time now to think not of revenge but of survival.

"How will we live without the herdbeasts and the Red Tongue?" asked Bira fearfully.

"There are other animals that we can eat," Thakur answered.

"But there are no herders to cull them for us or to keep them from running away." Bira turned her worried face to him.

"You can take them yourself. Haven't you ever stalked grasshoppers?"

"Yes, but that was a long time ago." The young Firekeeper cocked her head at him. "You mean, you can catch other animals that way? I never thought of that. I'm so used to eating from the clan kills."

Ratha quelled the scorn that started rising inside her at Bira's words. Once she too had been just as alarmed at the prospect of life outside the clan. She had been equally helpless until an Un-Named male taught her how to hunt and provide for herself. Hunger had made her an eager student, and she never forgot those lessons with Bonechewer, even though the thought of him still brought pain.

She knew that her life as clan leader had dulled her hunting skills, but practice could hone them again. Perhaps she could teach the rudiments to Thakur and Bira. The thought cheered her a little. At least she would have something else to think about other than her hatred of Shongshar.

"I lived apart from the clan for several seasons, Bira," she said slowly. "I learned how to hunt and take care of myself. I think I can teach you how to do the same."

Bira stared at her with respectful admiration, and Ratha suddenly felt warmed by the Firekeeper's gaze. She had almost forgotten what it meant to be looked up to for her own abilities rather than the fact she was clan leader. A life in exile, she thought, might have its compensations.

The little group set out later that same morning, with

most of the treelings riding on Bira and Ratha while Thakur and Aree took the lead. They left the pleasant shelter they had found by the fall and followed the stream farther up until they reached the spring that was its source. This was the end of clan territory in the direction of the setting sun. Shongshar would not seek them beyond this boundary.

At least not for a while, Ratha thought to herself.

They wound along the top of a forested ridge for the rest of the day and spent the night curled up together in dry leaves beneath a thicket. By midmorning of the following day, Thakur announced they had come far enough to avoid clan territory; he turned back downhill on the same side he had brought them up.

On the downgrade, their pace was much faster than it had been climbing, and by evening they were back on the plain with the setting sun behind them. On open land, the three could travel through the night. Morning found them approaching the redwood grove that Thakur had made his home during the mating season.

Once they reached it, Thakur showed Ratha and Bira the stream that flowed nearby and the den he had dug in the red clay beneath the roots of an old tree. The next task was to feed the treelings, who were growing cranky with hunger, having had only a few insects during the journey from clan territory. Aree led her brood up into the branches of the nearest laden tree while Thakur napped in the shade beneath and waited.

Ratha took Bira out into the open meadow and began to show her how to stalk quietly. They practiced on the big grasshoppers that clung to swaying fronds, and by the time the afternoon was over, Bira had caught several of the insects by herself. She couldn't quite bring herself to eat them, however, and Ratha ended up disposing of most of their catch.

When the two returned to Thakur, they found him covered with surfeited treelings and surrounded by fruit pits and gnawed cores. Some of the discards bore his toothmarks, and Ratha guessed that the treelings had shared their harvest. Neither she nor Bira wanted to try such strange food, so she set herself to hunting, leaving Bira behind with Thakur.

Her first attempts were unsuccessful, but on her next try, she caught a wounded ground-bird that had escaped another hunter and brought it back to her companions. The feathers made Bira sneeze, but she was too hungry to be fussy. The bird wasn't enough to fill their bellies, but Thakur had gnawed fruit while she had eaten all the grasshoppers. Bira ended up with most of the carcass and it was enough to satisfy her.

In the next few days, Ratha found herself assuming the role of major provider for the group. She caught small animals and birds for the others, and once managed to bring down a wild three-horn doe with some help from Thakur. The treelings flourished on the ripening fruit. The herding teacher, who admitted he was not much of a hunter, tried his skill at fishing in a nearby creek.

At first the task of providing for the group and feeding the treelings took up all of Ratha's time and attention. As practice rapidly sharpened her skills and strengthened unused muscles, she found her thoughts turning back to the clan. She would often wonder, as she followed the track of her prey through the grass, what was happening to the Named under Shongshar's leadership. If those thoughts distracted her and made her miss her kill, she snarled at herself and resolved to pay attention to what she was doing.

Despite herself, her curiosity grew, until she finally admitted that she could not turn her back on her people despite their betrayal of her. Bira, too, confessed that she hungered for the feel of familiar ground and the smells of those she knew.

Thakur was the most adamant about their need to leave the old life behind and not be tempted by any rash hopes of overthrowing Shongshar. Ratha finally gave up her attempts to convince him to come with her, to hide and watch the Named. Bira, however, was willing to come.

Together, they found a tree at the edge of clan land that was tall enough to overlook the meadow where the herdbeasts grazed. From this far height, the two could watch the activities of the herders without fear of being discovered. What they could see from their perch, however, only frustrated Ratha. The smells that the wind brought hinted that the herders were tense and uneasy, but whether they were worried about a lack of rain or the harshness of Shongshar's rule, she didn't know.

Ratha and Bira climbed down from their spying tree and started back to their own land. They hadn't gone far from the edge of clan teritory when Ratha heard a faint buzzing that grew louder and more ominous as they approached the sound.

A cloud of black flies hovered about a bush that stood to the side of the trail and beneath, in the shadows, something lay.

"A dead herdbeast, I think," said Bira, wrinkling her nose. "I can't smell it; the wind's not right."

Ratha peered at the still form. It didn't look the right shape for a dappleback or a three-horn, but she couldn't really tell. She normally didn't eat carrion, but she knew she shouldn't waste this opportunity. "The meat may still be good," she said to Bira and padded toward the bush.

"Don't taint your belly with this carcass, scavenger," said a hoarse voice, and a pair of dull yellow eyes opened in the shadowed darkness. "It's already begun to stink."

Ratha started at the well-remembered sarcasm in the voice and her jaw dropped in disbelief. "Fessran?"

The eyes gazed back at her, their brightness filmed over by fever and pain. She could hear harsh breathing above the drone of the flies. "Fessran?" she said again, coming closer.

Now she could see there was no fly-ridden dead herd-beast beneath the leaves, with Fessran crouched over it, as she had first thought. The limp form was Fessran herself and the flies were thick around her.

Ratha felt revulsion and sudden pity tighten her throat as she said, "You took the strike that was meant for me and I thought it killed you."

"It did. I'm just taking a long time to die." She gave Ratha an exhausted grin. "Remember, I guarded dapple-backs before I held the Red Tongue between my jaws. You and I both know that clan herders are hard to kill." She coughed and shuddered. "There was a carrion bird here before you came. I thought he'd be at me before I was dead. I'm glad you scared him away for a while." The eyes closed.

"We left you in the cavern . . ."

"I stayed there until Shongshar got tired of looking at me and had me dragged off clan ground," she said weakly and coughed again. "He made Cherfan do it. Poor herder, he gets all the nasty jobs. He tried to give me some meat, but I couldn't eat it and he looked so sad that I finally had to tell him to go." She paused and caught her breath. "You had better go too, Ratha."

Ratha wasn't listening. "Bira, hold the branches aside so I can see her wound," she told the young Firekeeper and the shadows slid back. She peered closer and swallowed to keep herself from gagging at the stench that rose from torn and ulcerated flesh. Shongshar's fangs had struck into Fessran's upper foreleg at the shoulder, driving through the leg itself and into her chest. Having her leg in the way was the only thing that saved her from an immediately fatal wound, but that death might have been better, Ratha thought, looking at Fessran's shrunken flanks and pain-wracked face.

Yet there was something in that face that told her Fessran wasn't ready to die, that if she had a chance, she would fight for her life with the same ferocity that had saved Ratha's. The wound itself wasn't that bad. What had weakened her was infection and starvation. If they could get her back to Thakur, his knowledge of healing might save her.

She knew that her friend read her intent, for Fessran shook her head slowly. "No, Ratha. Leave me here for the carrion birds. You have yourself and Bira to care for."

Ratha only laid back her ears at these words. "*Ptahh!* You were the one who said clan herders were hard to kill." She bent her head, seized Fessran's other forepaw, and dragged her out from beneath the bush. The flies swarmed about her in an angry cloud. "Crouch down, Bira," Ratha said before Fessran could pull away.

Trembling with pity, the little Firekeeper flattened herself near Fessran. Ratha gave the paw another tug.

"Ratha, you can't. I'm too heavy for her," Fessran protested as Bira wiggled herself underneath.

"You, Firekeeper leader?" Bira said over her shoulder and grinned at Ratha. "You're no heavier than the sticks I carry in my mouth or the fleas in my coat."

When Ratha had Fessran arranged so that she would not fall off, Bira stood up. Fessran gasped and hissed softly in pain. "All right?" Bira asked.

"No, but it's better than lying there with flies all over me," Fessran retorted.

Weakened as Fessran was, Ratha could see she seemed more herself than she had when they first discovered her. She felt a surge of hope that her friend would live.

Bira took a few cautious steps while Ratha walked beside her and steadied Fessran. When it became evident that Bira could carry her burden at a reasonable pace, she set off, with Ratha beside her. Fessran laid her head along Bira's neck and closed her eyes, letting her legs and tail dangle.

The journey was more painful for her than she would admit and, by the time they reached the redwood grove, she was moaning aloud and rolling her head back and forth. Blood and fluid from her wound trickled down Bira's side and seeped into the young Firekeeper's coat.

They put Fessran in Thakur's den beneath the redwoods and Ratha stayed with her while Bira ran to get Thakur. His astonishment at seeing her was only slightly less than his shock at seeing the ugliness of her wound. Immediately he set about gathering medicinal leaves, which Bira shredded and soaked in the stream before laying on the wound. He also took Aree with him to look for a type of fruit with a thick skin that had gone rotten and fuzzy. When he returned with these, he removed the skin. To Ratha's astonishment, he forced Fessran to swallow some of the moldy fuzz while he mixed the rest into the shredded poultice.

While he tended the wound, Ratha fed her friend with meat that she had chewed until it was almost liquid. Bira brought damp leaves from the stream to drip water onto Fessran's dry tongue.

For several days, she lay in the den like a lifeless thing, barely able to swallow or open her eyes. The food and water they gave her only seemed to be prolonging her end, and Ratha felt her hope slipping into desperation. The wound stank and oozed despite Thakur's poultices, and fever melted her away until she was little more than a skeleton.

Night after night, Ratha stayed beside Fessran, struggling not to fall into a doze for fear she would wake to look into her eyes and find the stare of death. With a fierce devotion, she fed her friend, even though the food often came back up.

And, finally, as they were at the point of giving up, Fessran began to rally. The swelling in the wound went down. It ceased oozing and crusted over. She was able to keep down the food that Ratha gave her and could suck on a wet leaf placed in her mouth.

She no longer lay limply on her side, but was able to roll onto her front, although she often grimaced with pain. She soon was able to take bits of meat and, with Ratha's aid, could stagger to the nearby stream to lap water.

As Fessran improved, Ratha was able to leave her and resume her task of hunting for the group. She continued teaching Bira her skill and before long the young female was making small kills of her own. Bira also accompanied

Ratha on forays to the spying tree, where they would hide and watch what went on in the meadow.

The clan culled more herdbeasts, but few of these were left to the herders. Most of the meat was taken by the Firekeepers and often dragged up the trail out of sight. Ratha strained for the sight or smell of Shongshar, but he never appeared in the meadow, even when the guard-fires were lit at dusk. She itched to know what was going on in the cave, and her anger conjured up images of him lolling before the Red Tongue, bloated with meat taken from the herders. Such thoughts made her growl between her teeth and shred the bark on the branch where she crouched.

Summer wore into autumn and the leaves began to turn and fall. One afternoon, after Ratha had helped Fessran back from the stream, the Firekeeper stretched herself out in the den and carefully licked the fur around the edge of her wound.

"Not too many of the Named have taken a bite like that and survived," Ratha observed.

"It was worth the pain. You and Thakur got away." Fessran fell silent for a while. "When I saw Shongshar about to kill you, I realized what he was. Before then, I lived in a daze. He used my fear of the fire-creature to lead me like a dappleback. He was so clever! Everything he said sounded right and even everything he did, until he bared his fangs to take your life."

"And almost took yours instead. I wanted to go back and rip Shongshar's throat out, but Thakur persuaded me not to try. Sometimes I think Thakur is the only one of us that has any sense."

"Yes," Fessran agreed and added, "Thank goodness."

They lolled their tongues at each other, and Ratha felt warmed by the quiet joy of renewed friendship. Yet not all of what Fessran had to say was pleasant. When Ratha asked her for her story, her eyes darkened and she told of the Firekeepers' arrogance, Shongshar's increasing gluttony and the fevered dances about the cave-fire. Already, she said, Shongshar had begun to use the terror of fire to expand clan holdings. More cubs were being trained as Firekeepers and the herders were being worked hard to provide enough meat for those who feasted in the Red Tongue's den.

As Ratha listened, her rage grew and she racked her mind for a way to wrest her power back from Shongshar. She knew that she was the one responsible for this change in her people. She had brought the gift of fire to the Named and with it had not only slain the old leader but ended the old laws and traditions that had governed the clan. Her rule had led them to triumph against the Un-Named, but she had failed to provide for the spiritual wants of her people, a hunger that grew and fostered Shongshar's rise.

Fessran began to speak of banding together to kill Shongshar. Once, Ratha would have been eager for such fierce talk, but time alone to think had shown her the truth of Thakur's words.

"No," she answered as Fessran stared at her with puzzled eyes. "Killing him would do no good. The Named want to crouch down before the Red Tongue and serve a leader who bears that power. If he were to die, his way would not end, for they would find another like him to rule in his place."

Her friend's eyes narrowed. "Suppose he were to die and the cave-fire along with him. Then if the Named had nothing to crouch down before, they would turn back to you."

"What good would my leadership do the clan without the Red Tongue to protect the herd? The Named have become too dependent on the fire-creature to survive without it."

"All of the Red Tongue need not die," answered Fessran. "The fire-creature in the cave is what gives him his power. Herders don't crouch down to guard-flames kept in the meadow or those kept in fire-lairs. They go to the cave. We must strike there."

The longer Ratha thought about Fessran's argument, the more convincing it sounded. If Shongshar lost the cave-fire, his influence would be severely crippled. "Some Firekeepers would also have to die, Fessran," said Ratha slowly. "The young ones, the cubs who know no way other than his. Your son, Nyang, would be one."

"He is more Shongshar's than mine," said Fessran bitterly. "It is my fault; I let Shongshar influence him and turn him into the little killer that he is. Even if he lived, he couldn't be trusted. No. I wouldn't let that turn me aside."

Ratha stared at her, looking deep into her eyes. "Are you saying you know of a way to destroy the fire-creature in the cave?"

"There is a big crack in the roof," said Fessran. "It draws the smoke up and out so that it doesn't fill the cavern. That's one reason we chose that cave for the Red Tongue's den." She paused. "The smoke comes out of several cracks above the falls. I've seen it when I've been up there."

"Are any of them wide enough to crawl through?"

"No, I don't think so," said Fessran.

"Then I don't see what good they are."

"Think," Fessran prodded her. "What is the greatest enemy of the Red Tongue? What was our reason for bringing the fire into the cavern?"

"The rain?" asked Ratha. "But how are you going to make it rain inside that cave?"

"Well, I'm not sure exactly how to do it, but the crack is close to the stream, and if smoke can come up, water can go down."

"How would you get the water from the stream into the crack?" Ratha cocked her head at Fessran.

"That's the part I don't know."

Ratha thought for a while. "Thakur might be able to help us. He often plays with mud and water when he's fishing."

When Thakur returned from the creek with his catch in his jaws, Ratha told him about Fessran's idea. At first, he seemed doubtful, but the longer he thought about it, the more he became convinced that the scheme might work. As for moving water from stream to cave, that could be done by digging a long trench in the earth from the stream to the cleft, making a path for the water to follow. He had dug such water-paths in the creekbank to trap fish.

"Do the cracks that lead into the cave lie above or below the stream?" he asked Fessran.

"In a little hollow where the stream bends before it reaches the falls," was her answer.

"Is the stream bank rocky or muddy there?"

Fessran thought it was muddy, but she wasn't sure. The only way to tell was to go and look.

Ratha turned to Thakur, who had begun to look doubtful again. "Herding teacher, this would give us a way to strike down the fire-creature and free our people from Shongshar. Will you work with us?"

Thakur agreed, and they began to plan a small expedition to the site to judge whether the idea would work. This time only Thakur and Ratha would go, along with Aree and Ratharee, leaving Bira to take care of Fessran and the rest of the treelings. If the plan was feasible, one of them would start digging while the other went back to the redwood grove to fetch Bira and Fessran, too, if she was well enough to travel.

Before Ratha left, she caught enough game so that Bira wouldn't have to hunt. When that was done, she and Thakur bid their companions farewell and set off.

To avoid trouble, they decided to return to clan ground by the same route they had come, skirting Shongshar's territory until they reached the spring that marked the border in the direction of the setting sun. They crossed over by night and hid until they were sure Shongshar wasn't patrolling this remote part of his ground. When daylight came, the two made their way downstream and Ratha soon recognized the bend that Fessran had described. They found the hollow by following the scent of smoke and discovered the maze of cracks from which it issued.

As Fessran had said, the stream lay slightly above the hollow, separated only by the grassy rise of its bank. If a deep enough channel could be dug, the stream could be turned from its course and rerouted down the hollow. The fissures that vented the cave lay near the bottom, so that the water filling the hollow would not have to rise far before it drained through them.

Thakur dug a hole at the top of the rise and found sandy clay as far down as he could reach. Ratha made another test excavation near the stream and came up with only a few stubborn rocks.

"This looks better than I'd thought," Thakur said after examining the results of her digging. "I had my doubts, but now I know that we can do it. I'll start while you fetch Fessran and Bira."

Within a few days, Ratha returned with the two others and the treelings. She sheltered them in small caves farther upstream they had previously used. Leaving Fessran and Bira to rest, she sought Thakur.

When she could find no trace of him or his work, she began to grow worried, but before long he appeared and pushed back some fallen branches and brush to show her the extent of the trench he had already dug.

"Whenever I leave, I hide it by laying branches across the top," he explained. "Then, even if any of the Fire-keepers comes along, they won't notice what we're doing."

"You've done a lot," said Ratha, impressed by the length and the depth of his excavation.

"There's much more to do and we'll have to hurry to finish before the rainy season starts," he replied and added almost mischievously, "Start digging, clan leader."

Despite her weariness from the journey, she got into the trench and began scraping away at the dirt in front of her. She dug all that day and late into the evening. She dug until her claws ached, scarcely noticing when Bira joined her. When she crawled out of the trench she staggered beneath a bush and collapsed into sleep.

The next day she dug and the day after that, and, when she was not digging, she hunted to feed the others who were devoting themselves even more to the task. Her life seemed to narrow, focusing only on the digging: guarding it, hiding it and extending it laboriously, day by day.

Thakur guided the work, making a pilot trench that Bira and Ratha deepened and widened. Fessran joined in, and, although her injury prevented her from attacking the hard-packed clay along with the other two, she could push aside the soil they threw between their legs, clear away brush and pull roots.

Even the treelings helped. Their clever paws could often dig a way around an embedded rock or break away a stubborn root. Aree sometimes acted as lookout, sitting in a tree that overhung the trench and screeching to warn of approaching intruders. The treelings groomed the dirt out of the diggers' fur, pulled caked clay from between aching pads and provided comfort and affection that was badly needed.

Ratha felt herself growing closer to Ratharee, who seemed to stay on her shoulder all the time, whether she was laboring in the trench or stalking game. The treeling knew to keep quiet during the hunt and to crouch and cling when Ratha sprang. Often Ratha would forget that Ratharee was there until a little voice murmured in her ear or small fingers began to clean her fur.

Fessran and Bira also chose treeling companions. The injured Firekeeper had become friendly with Ratharee's older sibling. At first she had viewed the treelings with mixed emotions and had been reluctant to take one, but once the relationship had begun, it grew with amazing rapidity until Fessran couldn't be separated from her new companion. Bira chose the younger male of Aree's brood, leaving Thakur with only Aree herself and her elder son. Bira called her treeling Biaree, imitating Ratha's way of naming them.

Days passed, and the trench was gradually extended

from the hollow where it had begun over the rise to the stream. It became deep enough so that someone could walk in it with only the tips of their ears showing above the edge, and wide enough to turn around in. Ratha and her companions interrupted their work only to eat, sleep and relieve themselves. Each section of the spillway was covered over with branches and brush as it was completed, so that if intruders threatened, the diggers only had to conceal the open trench they were working in.

Sunset came a little earlier each day, giving them less light to work by. Falling leaves drifted into the trench and had to be cleared out. Ratha sensed that it was nearly time for the clan's mating season to begin, but neither she nor her female companions showed signs of going into heat. She vowed to herself that even if she did, she was going to stay at the bottom of the trench and use her restlessness to dig. Fessran and Bira agreed with her, saying that, if any of them felt the onset of the mating urge, they could send Thakur away to fish and provide food while they continued to work. The layout of the spillway was now complete, with two pilot trenches running side by side to mark the width of the remaining section to be dug.

One morning Ratha and Bira were widening the side of the channel when Ratha felt something sting her nose. She looked up to see gray clouds rolling above the trees; another drop struck her between the eyes.

"The rains are coming early," said Thakur, leaning into the trench and alternately glancing down at her and up at the sky.

"How far are we from the stream bank?" she asked, lifting her nose above the piles of dirt on the edge.

"A few tail-lengths. We're going to have to dig deeper, though, to cut through the bank and make the water run this way."

She sighed and went back to work.

Overhead, the clouds grumbled and the rain began. At first it was light and helped by softening the ground so that the work went faster. As it grew into a pelting down-pour, the bottom of the trench became a bog. The diggers fought to keep their footing on the slick clay and fre-quently fell into puddles or accidentally spattered each other with the pawfuls of mud they flung aside. Their small companions began to look less like treelings and more like soggy mudballs.

At the end of the day, Ratha would crawl shivering from the trench, her coat soaked, her underside and flanks grimy with clay and gravel. Once she was under shelter, Ratharee made a determined attempt to groom her, but the treeling was often so exhausted that she fell asleep when she had barely begun. Ratha was so tired, she didn't care.

The work grew more difficult and the task seemed end-less. Sometimes Ratha, in her haze of fatigue, couldn't remember what the purpose of it was. She felt as though she had spent her life scraping away at this wretched hole and would do so for the rest of her existence. When at last Thakur leaned down into the trench again and cried, "Stop!," she paid no attention to him and kept on digging mechanically until water began seeping through the gravel and soil at her feet.

She felt Thakur drop into the ditch beside her, seize her scruff and shake her. "Ratha, stop! We're finished. If you go any farther, the water-path will flood before we're ready."

She blinked, trying to pull herself out of her daze. She scrambled out of the trench after Thakur and saw that he was right. Only the remaining thin wall of earth held back the stream. When the time came, they would dig at the embankment to weaken it until it broke, sending the flow down the spillway, into the hollow and down the cracks that vented the cave below. The cave-fire would perish in a rush of water, and those who tended it would be swept away.

Despite her exhaustion, Ratha felt a surge of triumph. She was ready. Now all the remained was to wait.

CHAPTER 18

THE SUN HID for days behind a heavy bank of clouds, and the rain fell without ceasing. The stream began to swell, surging and cutting away at its banks until Ratha feared the wall of earth at the high end of the spillway would not hold it back. Now she crouched on the rise above the stream bank, watching the swirling water with anxious eyes.

The break had to be controlled, Thakur had said. If the packed earth gave way too soon or in the wrong place, the rushing water could destroy the channel and race down the hillside, missing the hollow. All their work would be useless if that happened.

Ratharee huddled on the ground beneath her, seeking

shelter from the rain in the warmth between her forepaws and her breast. Ratha could feel the little body shiver.

"It won't be long now, Ratharee," she said softly, feeling the treeling's paws on her forefeet. "Bira's gone down to spy on the cave. She'll be back soon."

As she waited for Bira, she found herself thinking about Shongshar, as she had often done during the past days. At first her mind had been clouded with hate. Once the cave-fire was destroyed and his rule ended, she vowed to force the Firekeepers to change their arrogant ways. No one in the clan would speak Shongshar's name without a hiss. Both his memory and his ways would be buried.

Yet she now realized that as ruthless and cruel as he had become, Shongshar had greater vision than she had. He was right: she had left the true understanding of the Red Tongue's power to him, and thereby forfeited her leadership. The veneration of fire had thrust her people into debasement and a savagery previously unknown among their kind, but it also fed a hunger of the spirit, a need that could neither be ignored nor denied.

He was also right that the Named were pushed beyond themselves by the awesome presence of the Red Tongue. Not only did gazing into the fire inspire them to greater strength and courage, it gave them the vision to seek beyond the limits of their everyday life for a sense of meaning. Even Shongshar's dream of extending his rule beyond clan ground was as inspired as it was arrogant, she admitted grudgingly.

As much as she hoped to obliterate all traces of his rule from among her people, she knew some of the things he had done could not be changed. This realization had forced her to put aside her hate long enough to see that not everything the Firekeepers had done under his rule was wrong. Storing wood and sheltering the source-fire in the cave were sound ideas, even though they had been turned to self-serving purposes.

If a large shelter such as the cave had been located in the meadow instead of far up the creek trail, it would have been more difficult to misuse. Had the Firekeepers been made to understand that the Red Tongue's power was a gift for all to share, perhaps it might have been more difficult for Shongshar to lead them astray. And if she had understood the need of her people to belong to a power greater than themselves and used it for good instead of turning it aside, then Shongshar might not have been able to turn the clan against her.

Ratha heard the slap of wet pads and caught the smell of Bira's soggy pelt. The shapes of the young female and her treeling appeared through the rain.

"Most of the Firekeepers are inside," she panted as she crouched beside Ratha. "Shongshar is having a great feast in the cave. Where are Thakur and Fessran?"

"They're coming." Ratha shivered with cold and impatience.

When the other two arrived, Bira told them the news. They looked at each other with rising excitement and then all eyes turned to Ratha.

"Take Ratharee, Fessran," she said and sprang onto the top earth dike holding back the stream. Dirt flew into the foaming water. She attacked the soil as if it were Shongshar's throat; rage made her paw strokes more powerful.

"They'll be starting . . . to dance . . . around the Red Tongue . . . soon," she growled as she redoubled her efforts. Brown water began to trickle through the channel between her feet. She was turning to Thakur with a grin when she felt the earth give way beneath her.

Her triumph quickly turned to terror as the earth wall broke and toppled. She threw herself to one side, twisting and scrabbling for a clawhold. She landed on her belly, her hindquarters and tail in the surging flood that spilled through the break. As the wall crumbled the current grew stronger, tugging at her hindquarters. She splashed and kicked with frantic strength, knowing that if she fell beneath the pouring water, she would never fight her way to the surface. She would be carried like a leaf down into the frothing cauldron that would fill the hollow. The Red Tongue would have its revenge even before it died.

That thought gave her the added strength to stretch farther up the bank and drive her claws into harder ground. Her shoulder muscles cramped with the effort of dragging her body from the hungry current. Part of the bank broke away beneath one forepaw and she dangled, held by the claws of the other. She felt teeth seize her flailing paw and grunted as she was yanked up until her chest and then her belly lay on the edge.

Someone caught her scruff, someone else grabbed a hind paw, and treeling hands were on her tail. She was hauled, dragged and rolled away as the rest of the bank caved in, threatening to sweep away both her and her rescuers. When they finally reached safe ground, she could only lie and pant while the others looked anxiously at her.

"I'm all right," she gasped, struggling to her feet. "See what's happened." She shook herself, though it was useless in the heavy rain, and staggered to where the others stood.

Water from the rain-swollen stream coursed into the channel, washing away the remains of the earthen wall. The flood widened and deepened its new course, eating farther into the original streambed and diverting more and more water into the spillway. Ratha and Bira ran along the edge of their ditch, following the foaming wave down to the bottom of the hollow. The strength of the current was enough to send the muddy water fountaining up onto the slope of the hollow and right into the cracks venting the cave.

"We've done it!" Ratha roared to Bira as they galloped back to the top where Fessran and Thakur waited.

"We certainly have," said Thakur as she reached him. "Look. The stream's left its old path entirely." He pointed with his paw toward the streambed below the spillway opening. Only a small trickle of water ran between puddles in the sand.

Above the roar of water surging into the channel, Ratha caught the sound of shrieks and cries drifting up from far below.

"The cave-fire must be dead!" she cried, leaping up. "Now we strike against Shongshar!"

She led the four of them down past the new lake that was filling the hollow, to the trail that led to the bottom of the waterfall. She noticed that the sound of the fall was gone. Instead, the noise of falling water came from the cave that had once been the Red Tongue's den. A torrent gushed from the entrance, washing away a portion of the trail that ran beside the stream and cutting its way back to fill the now-empty streambed.

Even as they watched, a body rode out on the flow, tumbling over rocks and boulders until it was finally pushed to one side and left. Ratha could see others, some lying limp and still in the rain, some trying to crawl away from the growing cataract.

Charred logs that hurtled out on the flood about the entrance gave evidence that the cave-fire had been drowned and washed away. The conspirators gazed at each other, awed by the destruction.

Ratha's imagination gave her an image of what the inside of the cave had been like when the water came pouring in. First, a small dribble that hissed into steam when it struck the Red Tongue and startled the dancers. Then more rivulets falling from the ceiling, glinting in the firelight. The dancers would have stopped, laying back their ears and snarling at this strange invasion. And when the full force of the flood hit the great fire and plunged the cave into sudden darkness, she could almost hear the howls and screams above the echoing roar that grew louder and louder....

Some would have tried to flee the cave in a panic near madness, guessing that the earth itself had turned against them for their wickedness in worshiping the Red Tongue. She could imagine that terror in the eyes of the half-drowned Firekeepers.

"It must have been terrible," said Bira softly, saying what Ratha saw in the eyes of the two others.

"Let's find Shongshar," she said roughly and turned away.

They found him farther downstream, in a small gorge beside the trail. The rush of water had carried him with it, tumbling and turning him until at last it flung him aside. Now he lay, a sodden mass of silver fur, among the boulders at the bottom.

Carefully Ratha made her way down into the gorge,

followed by the others. If Shongshar was dead, he shouldn't be left to rot in the stream and taint the water. He should be taken elsewhere and buried. And if he wasn't dead, she should know.

He remained so still as she approached that she was convinced life had gone from him. She was about to tell Thakur to take Shongshar's tail in his jaws when Shongshar's eyes suddenly cracked open. With a gasp, Bira skittered back, bumping into Fessran.

Shongshar's eyes widened and focused on Ratha. She felt a sudden chill that was not just the wind on her wet pelt.

"Your rule is ended, Shongshar," she said, trying to keep the tremor from her voice. "The Red Tongue in the cave has been destroyed and the Firekeepers are too frightened to listen to you again."

"Then it was you who sent the angry water into the cave," he hissed and drew a shuddering breath.

"Yes."

"You have grown great indeed if water moves itself to do your will," he said hoarsely. "The weaker power must yield to the stronger. That is the law of all things, clan leader. I offer you my throat for your fangs." He rolled his head back as he spoke.

"Be careful!" Thakur hissed beside her. Behind her she could hear Fessran growl, "Kill him for me, Ratha."

But Ratha stepped back from him. "No. There has been enough death among us. I offer you this, Shongshar. You may leave clan ground with your life, if you never return."

"You offer me nothing then," he snarled weakly.

"You say there is nothing for you outside the clan. What about your cubs?"

His eyes narrowed, and orange blazed between the lids. His lips drew back from his fangs as he spat. "You are crueler than I am, Ratha. You killed them. The thought of their deaths only left me when I gazed into the heart of the Red Tongue, and now that is gone, you torment me again with their memory."

"Would you believe me if I told you I didn't kill your cubs? Thakur and I took them off clan ground and left them in a place where they could find food and water. They might still be alive."

Shongshar looked at her and she saw a faint hope warring with rage in his eyes. He sought Thakur. "Does she speak truth, herding teacher?"

"Yes," Thakur replied.

"You couldn't have told me, could you?" Shongshar said bitterly, turning his gaze back to Ratha.

"I couldn't trust you. Listen, when you are ready to leave clan ground, I'll tell you where we left them."

Shongshar sank back, a strange glaze over his eyes. "You should have trusted me then, clan leader . . . it's too late now."

Ratha barely heard Thakur's warning cry before a fierce blow struck the side of her head, sending her reeling. Shongshar was suddenly on top of her, raking her sides with his claws. She writhed underneath him, heaving and bucking, trying to dodge the plunging teeth. A fang scored her side and she lashed up, dragging her claws across his cheek.

"I offered to let you go . . . to find your lost cubs," she gasped. She twisted underneath him, ignoring the rocks that bruised her back.

"What good would it do me to search for them now?" he hissed. "If they were as witless as you believed, they wouldn't care who fathered them. And if they weren't, they have been gone from me too long to know me."

She understood then that hate had worked inside him too long for anything to turn it aside. The fierce glow of his eyes was the fire of madness. "No, Ratha," he hissed, baring his fangs in front of her face. "All I want from you now is your death or mine."

Again he strained his head back for a killing downslash. At the instant his throat lay exposed, Thakur struck. The momentum of the herding teacher's attack thrust Shongshar aside from Ratha. She scrambled to her feet as Fessran and Bira leaped to Thakur's aid.

Fessran made up for the handicap of her injury by the intensity of her rage. Shongshar was bleeding from many wounds by the time the three bore him down, but their combined strength could scarcely hold him.

"All right, Shongshar," Ratha panted. "You have a choice. Either you leave clan ground now, or your life ends here."

His only answer was a lunge at Ratha. Thakur cast her a look of despair that told her Shongshar had made his decision, and there was nothing the herding teacher could do about it.

"You are going to kill me," Shongshar said, narrowing his eyes at Thakur. "That is a bitter thing, to have to kill one who was a friend. If you don't, I will bury my teeth in her. Choose which one of us you will grieve for, herding teacher."

Again he lunged for Ratha, nearly throwing off his captors. They seized him, throwing him back. Thakur opened his jaws for the killing bite.

"No," Ratha said. "I brought him among us. I will take him to the dark trail."

She felt the herding teacher tremble as he moved aside for her. He looked at her, his eyes dark with grief. "Be quick," he said and stared away.

When it was done and Shongshar lay still, Ratha lifted her head with a deep weariness that seemed to fill her. She stared down at the blood oozing onto the silver fur, as the others backed away from the body.

"We will carry him into the meadow and place him beneath the tree where Bonechewer died," she said softly. "He deserves at least that much."

"Ratha!" The harshness in Thakur's voice jerked her gaze from Shongshar. Fessran was looking up at the rim of the gorge, her tail starting to wag. Angry eyes glared down. The Named were all about them, descending the steep slope of the gorge on both sides. It was too late to run or to hide Shongshar's body. Ratha knew she would either have to win the clan over or fight.

She felt Thakur edge against her, protecting Bira between himself and Fessran. The bitter smell of vengeance-hunger filled the stream as the Named crept down into the gorge.

"It's a bad place for a fight," Thakur growled softly.

"Stay together," Fessran hissed. "To reach any of us, they'll have to kill us all."

Ratha narrowed her eyes at the pack. She sensed that the herders among them did not seem as vengeful as the Firekeepers; in fact the latter had to bully the herders into sullen complacency.

"There is the one who murdered our leader and teacher! Tear out her throat!" cried a Firekeeper and he clawed a herder, who flinched and growled, "Yes, tear out her throat!"

"Let her taste the same meat she gives to others!" cried someone else among the herders.

"*Ptahh!*" Ratha spat back. "You herders know the meat he gave you. He dragged away your beasts to glut himself and those who served him while leaving you nothing. Why do you howl for him?"

"He gave us power and strength," roared one. "He gave us the dance in the cave," howled another.

"The dance," said Ratha. "And was that dance ever for herders? Were the ones who worked to feed the Firekeepers ever allowed to come before the cave-fire to feast and share in the celebration?"

The herders exchanged looks with each other, despite the Firekeepers' prodding. "No," muttered one. "They said our coats were too dirty and that we must watch from a distance and be grateful that the Red Tongue would even permit us in the cave."

Other mutterings broke out, and Ratha could hear more complaints being spoken against Shongshar's attitude toward those who tended the clan's animals.

"I'm glad Shongshar's dead," roared someone else, and with a start Ratha recognized Cherfan's voice. "I'm tired of crouching to those singe-whiskered fools and hearing that we herders aren't worthy to approach the Red Tongue."

Heads turned among the herders and more voices joined Cherfan's until they broke from the rest of the clan and crowded around Ratha. Cherfan faced the Firekeepers and bellowed, "All right, now we'll see how brave you are in a fair fight!"

But Ratha could see that the Firekeepers still held the advantage. Although there were more herders in the meadow, Cherfan had no way of summoning their help without forcing a confrontation. And whether the sides were matched or not did not matter to Ratha. This battle would cost the clan heavily in lives no matter who won.

"If she wins, she will forbid us to crouch before the fire creature or offer ourselves in the dance," she heard one Firekeeper growl to another. Muttering spread among them and one yowled, "Attack now! She has killed the fire-creature in the cave. She will keep the Red Tongue from rising again."

"No!" cried Ratha, turning to face him. "You are wrong!"

Even Thakur and Fessran stared at her in astonishment as she waved her tail for silence. "Hear me, Firekeepers," she said. "I understand your wish to crouch and dance before the Red Tongue. I once thought that was wrong and should be stopped, but I know better now. I killed the cave-fire because it was being misused." She paused, looking into their eyes. "Tell me yourselves. Was it right to look down upon the herders and take their beasts when your bellies were already bloated? Or to keep them from the cave unless they brought you meat?"

Several Firekeepers lowered their heads and stared down at their paws. "No," Ratha continued. "Shongshar did wrong by making you believe that serving the fire-creature made you more deserving than the rest. He used your belief to make you do fierce and cruel things you would not have done. That is why he died."

A Firekeeper raised his head. "Then you will allow us to honor the Red Tongue as well as use it to guard the herds?"

"Yes. I have said nothing against honoring the fire-creature itself. Listen. This is what I will do. We will enlarge one of the old fire-lairs to make an earth-cave in the meadow where the source-fire may be kept. There dry wood can be stored and the fire will be safe from rain. It will be guarded, but anyone, Firekeeper or herder, may enter for warmth, and they may crouch and lower their whiskers before the fire, if they wish."

"I don't think that's enough," growled another Firekeeper, glaring at Ratha. "Shongshar allowed only us to approach Red Tongue and crouch before it. The herders should tend their dapplebacks."

Yowls and hisses rose from the herders and the fur on their napes began to lift. Ratha feared that she might not be able to avert a fight.

"Listen to me, both of you. I brought the Red Tongue to the clan for all to share. The Firekeepers were created so that their skills could benefit the rest of us. Herders, the Firekeepers need you as much as you need them. Neither of you can survive without the skill of the others. If you follow me, I will see that both herders and Firekeepers share the fire-creature in a way that is good for both."

Again mutters broke out from the Firekeepers. The one who had challenged Ratha tried to speak again, but was silenced by his companions. She waited until the Firekeepers had stopped scuffling and speaking among themselves. "Clan leader," the first one said, "most of us think that what you have suggested is wise. But we need our own leader. We would like Fessran to return to us."

"I think that can be done," said Ratha as she turned to her friend and said in a lower voice, "Now that you know the pitfalls along this path, I can trust you to tread it with care."

A few Firekeepers separated themselves from their companions and glared at Ratha. "I still don't like it," complained the same one who had objected before. "You think that Shongshar was wrong to take meat from the herders and give it to us? We need more than they do. We have to be strong. What's wrong with that?"

With a roar Fessran sprang forward. "I'll tell you what's wrong with that, you greedy wretch!" He skittered away as she glared at the others in his group. "What Ratha offers is fair to all, and I intend to support her. Either you obey my orders, or you leave the Firekeepers. Is that clear?"

With sullen growls they reluctantly agreed.

To pull Shongshar's body up out of the gorge took the efforts of Ratha and her companions. When that was done, she sent Thakur and Fessran to search for other survivors of the disaster who might have fled and were now in hiding. Gradually they began to come back, their coats soaked and their eyes haunted. Some coughed and wheezed from the water in their lungs, while others walked stiffly, pained by sprains and bruises. When they were all assembled, Ratha led them down to the meadow.

Fessran and Bira took care of the half-drowned Firekeepers, treating them like a large litter of disobedient but still-loved cubs. Fessran made them dry themselves by the fire, a new blaze that had been lit from the fire-lairs. Bira soothed those who still trembled from their memories.

Ratha found the bodies of those who had died in the flood and helped to bring them to be laid under grave-trees at the edge of clan ground. Among the dead was the herder Shoman. Another, as she had feared, was Fessran's son, Nyang.

Some of the more wrathful herders wanted to tear Shongshar's body and scatter his bones, but Ratha sternly forbade them from approaching him. Carefully and respectfully, she and Thakur carried the body through the meadow and laid it beneath Bonchewer's grave-tree.

In the following days, she and Fessran reorganized the Firekeepers, reducing their number and sending some to be retrained as herders. Now that she had control of the Red Tongue again, she could encourage Thakur and the others who had treelings to resume training them in the art of caring for fire. She was pleased to learn that Aree had not forgotten her careful lessons and the young treelings still retained much of what they had learned. She and Ratharee joined in with the others and soon were spending many of their evenings learning what treeling paws could do.

They had many spectators, for those in the clan who did not have treelings were drawn by curiosity. There was still some uneasiness about having such creatures tend the Red Tongue, but Ratha sensed that it was diffuse and no longer the threat it had been during Shongshar's rise to power. She shared Ratharee with those who wished to try working with a treeling and encouraged Thakur, Bira and Fessran to do the same.

As Ratha lifted the first pawful of earth from the threshold of the old fire-lair, she hesitated before throwing it aside. Despite her words to the Firekeepers, she felt she had set her feet in Shongshar's pawprints and hoped she would have the strength not to take the trail he had followed.

She felt Ratharee on her shoulder, turned her head to nuzzle the treeling and felt calmer. The creature's gentle touch eased the loneliness that sometimes came over her even when she was close to her own kind. Ratharee couldn't speak, but she seemed to say as much with her nimble hands and bright, wise eyes as the Named did with words.

The treeling shared much more than the skill of her hands. She was a companion who never questioned or judged. Her presence seemed to lessen Ratha's fierce need to prove herself to others, and she felt herself gaining a stability of mind that she had not known before.

When she was directing Ratharee in a task such as laying out kindling, she often felt that the treeling knew what she wanted before she nudged her arms or gave the clicking sounds that she followed. The understanding between them grew less that of one creature serving another and became a partnership. In concentrating on a task, the bond between them grew so strong that she and Ratharee were one being with shared abilities beyond those of either partner.

She also realized that the relationship was more equal than she had first thought. While she experienced the treeling's dexterity as if it were her own, she sensed that her companion was gaining knowledge treelings had never had. She gave Ratharee her strength and her speed as well as her ability to see at night. Her intelligence too she shared, although she often wondered, when she looked into the startling depths of Ratharee's eyes, whether treelings might have a cleverness of their own that was equal to that of the Named, even though it was different.

When she ventured to ask her companions how they felt about their treelings, she found she was not alone in her discovery. Even those of the Named who had only watched or worked with them for brief periods seemed to benefit from the contact.

Now she scraped away another pawful of dirt as others

of the clan began to dig with her. She glanced at Thakur, alongside her, and noticed that Aree was looking a bit bulgier than she had been.

"She's pregnant again," said Thakur with a grin. "Don't ask me how she did it."

Ratha continued her task, feeling happy. Soon there would be more treelings for those of the clan who wanted them. And nearly everybody did.

She sensed this was a coming change for her people, a change more subtle but no less powerful than the bringing of the Red Tongue to the clan. But unlike the use and worship of fire, which raised savage instincts, the growing partnership of the Named with treelings seemed to waken the gentler part of their nature, giving it strength.

It gave her a strange feeling of hope, though she almost doubted it herself as she continued to dig, but it refused to leave her mind. She found herself watching her friends to see whether the change she imagined was real, and she found that it was. Even Fessran, the one who had resisted the treelings and only taken a companion after her illness, admitted she felt the effect. She was no less irascible and her comments were as pointed as ever, but her sudden flares of temper, which made others wary of her, were gone.

Perhaps it was this that gave Ratha a true hope that she could lead her people along a new path. The treelings would serve the Named not only by caring for fire with the skill of their fingers, but by lessening the feelings of loneliness and hunger for those things of the spirit that had driven the Named to frenzied obedience to the Red Tongue.

* * *

The flicker of firelight lit the earthen walls and cast a glow over the wet grass of the meadow. A light rain fell in the dusk, but the source-fire was safe in its shelter. The den had been dug deep and well, with holes to vent the smoke and allow the flame to draw. A raised floor of packed earth had been made to hold the fire above any water that might seep in, and an adjacent chamber had been dug in which to stack and dry wood. It was now half-filled with remains of the cave woodpile, pieces of which had been recovered and dried before the watch-fires.

A little while before, Ratharee had ridden on Ratha's back, bearing the brand to kindle this new source-fire. Now as the flame grew and crackled, it lit the faces of the herders and Firekeepers who gathered before the den.

"Now the Red Tongue's protection will never fail!" cried Fessran, and to Ratha's surprise, she gave a joyous leap into the air with her treeling on her back. She landed a little awkwardly, for her injured foreleg was still weak, but she gave Ratha a grin and jumped up again.

The sense of celebration was contagious, and everyone began circling the glowing mouth of the fire-shelter, their coats gleaming in the rain. They sprang and whirled. Even Thakur joined in, with Aree bouncing between his shoulders. It was all the treeling could do to hold on, but the shine in her eyes was excitement, not fear.

Only Ratha held herself back. The circle of dancers seemed to be overlaid by another image that floated before her eyes. That too was a dance, the terrifying frenzy of those who threw themselves into the heated air in the cave, whose eyes shimmered with cruelty and the worship of the fierce light in their center. It was all before her again, the sound, the smell and the racing of her heart until she wanted to cry aloud to end it.

The fire-creature of her dream was there too, rising out of the flame's center with a shape that was and was not the form of the Named. But as it reared up to claw at the roof of the cave, it seemed to falter and sink back down as the roar of the fire grew muted and the flame itself dwindled . . . until it was just a glow from the mouth of an earthen den and the dancers about her were her people and her friends. The shimmer in their eyes was joy, and the firelight shone on their power and grace.

Yes, they could dance before the Red Tongue, giving thanks for the light, the warmth and the protection it gave. And they could see the beauty in its strength and rejoice in that without seeking to make it a weapon for others to fear.

And suddenly the dance changed. The treelings had joined in, leaping in a counter-circle from one dancer to the next as if weaving them together.

In a moment, Ratharee sprang from Ratha's back into the ring of dancers. Rain sparkled on her pelt as she scampered along Thakur's back and launched herself onto Fessran's withers.

"The only way you'll get her back is to join in," yowled Bira as Ratharee bounced onto the young Firekeeper as she danced around the circle.

And Ratha did.

Later, when exhaustion laid the Named and treelings together in a sprawl amid the soggy grass, Ratha lifted her head wearily to see happy lolling tongues all around her.

"You've got the longest one," she teased, swatting Fessran playfully. "Stuff it back in your mouth." The treelings scampered out of the way as the two wrestled like cubs and then broke away, panting at each other.

The rain stopped. Those of the clan picked themselves up and went back to their duties or their dens. Fessran and Thakur rose together and he offered to walk back with Ratha to her lair.

"No, I want to stay here awhile," she said. She watched them leave and listened to the far-off lowing of herdbeasts and the muted crackle of the source-fire in its shelter. Soon she would have to call someone to watch over it while she went to her den, but for now she could be alone.

She felt Ratharee climb onto her and curl up on her flank. She yawned and sensed a quiet contentment creeping over her. Although she and her people had suffered much, they were still alive and together. They would mourn the ones who died, Shoman, Nyang and the Fire-keepers. And Shongshar? Perhaps only she would visit his bones beneath the pine.

Yes, I will mourn him, she thought. *It was grief that made him seek such a dark trail. And he has taught me a lesson that I will not forget, even though it is bitter. I must learn to feed the hunger of my people that does not ask for food, for I know now that a leader does not rule only by strength and will.*

And she lay thinking, with the orange glow casting her shadow on the grass until it was nearly dawn. Again she had found a new way for herself and her people, and this time she would lead them not only with strength and persistence, but the care of her newly found wisdom. She lifted her head and narrowed her eyes at the sun as it rose over the trees and spilled its first light on clan ground.